MW00365781

Monologues from the Makom

Intertwined Narratives of Sexuality, Gender, Body Image, and Jewish Identity

Edited by Rivka Cohen,
Naima Hirsch,
Sara Rozner Lawrence,
Sarah J. Ricklan,
and Rebecca Zimilover

Teaneck, New Jersey

MONOLOGUES FROM THE MAKOM ©2020 Rebecca Cohen. All rights reserved. No part of this book may be used or reproduced in any manner whatsoever without written permission except in the case of brief quotations embodied in critical articles and reviews.

Cover Painting: *In* by Amalya Sherman
(Instagram @amalya.sherman)

Published by Ben Yehuda Press
122 Ayers Court #1B
Teaneck, NJ 07666

http://www.BenYehudaPress.com

To subscribe to our monthly book club and support independent Jewish publishing, visit patreon.com/BenYehudaPress

Ben Yehuda Press books may be purchased at a discount by synagogues, book clubs, and other institutions buying in bulk. For information, please email markets@BenYehudaPress.com

ISBN13: 978-1-934730-04-1

A version of "Private Places" appeared in the JOFA Blog.
A version of "You Shouldn't Have" appeared in the JOFA Blog.
A version of "What They Don't Tell You About Getting Married at 19" appeared on Hevria.
"I have been trying to write this all week" was previously submitted for publication in Staunch, the publication of which has been delayed indefinitely.

20 21/ 10 9 8 7 6 5 4 3 2 1   20200625

With gratitude to our mothers and grandmothers
for the world they built for us,

We dedicate this collection to our children, grandchildren,
and every generation to come —
May you always know strength and love.

Monologues from the Makom

Contents

דרש רב עוירא בשכר נשים צדקניות שהיו
באותו הדור נגאלו ישראל ממצרים

*Rav Avira taught: In the merit **of the righteous
women** that were in that generation, the Jewish
people were redeemed from Egypt.*
—Sotah 11b

What was so righteous about the women of that generation
that by their merit, the Jewish people were redeemed from
Egypt? In a vivid picture painted in Sotah 11b, we learn that
the women of that time, despite the darkness and hopelessness of their enslavement, initiated sexual activity with their
partners, making it possible for future generations to continue. Furthermore, this initiative infused a sense of life, hope,
and playfulness into Jewish homes at a time of extreme pain
and narrowness. Ultimately, our people were redeemed and
we began our journey to the Promised Land. On the way, as
the time came to build the Mishkan in the Wilderness, the
people rushed forward with precious donations. Rashi notes
that the women of Israel came as a group to offer one thing
in sisterhood: their mirrors. The very mirrors they used to
enhance their beauty and play flirtatious games with their
partners to increase desire. Moshe responds unfavorably, and
rejects them. Mirrors? They aren't modest. They serve the
evil inclination. They make us think evil, non-holy thoughts.
They aren't an appropriate centerpiece for our Holy Places.

But Hashem responds:

א״ל הקב״ה- קבל! כי אלו חביבין עלי מן
הכל שעל ידיהם העמידו הנשים צבאות רבות
במצרים.

God said to him: "Accept them, for these are
dearer to me than all the rest, for it is with
them that the women raised many congregations
[this is the meaning of 'the women who congre-
gate' in the verse] in Egypt.
—*Rashi on Shemot 38:8*

The *Monologues from the Makom* book is a brave volume, a
set of unique and holy mirrors. It is an extraordinary collection of women's voices coming from a place of the feminine,
the wild, the intimate, and the bold. Just as the women in
Egypt took risks to own their femininity and sexuality, these
writings come from a deep place where women take control
over their own voices and stories. Reading these pieces feels
like a privilege, a tiny glimpse into 32 mirrors. Within each
one, we of course see the reflection of the writer; but readers
will also see themselves. Women who read these pieces will
likely identify deeply with at least several of these works.

Why do I say that the volume is brave? Moshe's reaction,
which is one of resistance, fear, and negativity is familiar to
many of us. Many women worry about what will happen if
they talk about sex, about their bodies, about consent or lack
thereof. Some of us have already suffered consequences in
our communities when we shared honestly about our most
intimate moments. We've seen "Moshes" reject our mirrors.

You're too much, it's not modest, it's not right. This teaching of Chazal is crucial, however, to understanding how we should be receiving this sacred book. Hashem reminds us that ***Elu Chavivin Alai Min HaKol***—it is precisely what these stories can offer that are the dearest. It is because of these mirrors, which reflect pain, joy, love, and life—that the redemption will begin and we can raise up our communities and one another.

I know the redemptive power of these stories. As an Orthodox woman who also serves as a clergy member, I've had the opportunity to work with women in the halakhically observant community in the most intimate of spaces—watching tears streaming down cheeks into the mikveh, laughing and learning in groups in living rooms, or navigating a way to a new balance when a woman brings life into the world or suffers a loss. What is reflected in these stories is stunning and redemptive. I am blessed to be a sacred story bank for the inner lives of women, and I'm grateful to the writers and editors for opening up this world to a larger number of people.

Over the years, I've accumulated so many important books. I always gravitate towards two different genres when I'm looking for new books to add to my collection—Judaica and Women's Studies. I take great pride in the library I've built, which incorporates everything from the oldest edition of *Our Bodies, Ourselves* to the newest edition of Rav Moshe Feinstein's responsa literature. The works that move me the most, however, are the ones which sit and serve as bridges between the two sections. The ones which marry the two worlds of the sacred feminine and the Holy Torah. I am so proud that this collection of essays will sit on that important shelf.

When you peruse this volume, especially if you have lived your life identified as a woman, you might find you are *experiencing* this book as opposed to reading it. It will bring up instances in your life that might make you angry or sad or joyous and tingly. I invite the reader to find themselves in these works, and feel that your experience is reflected in the world. Some essays may feel overwhelmingly resonant. Others may seem far removed from your experience. Regardless, take a moment to honor each piece as a beautiful story in its own right—a mirror that deserves to be in our holiest of spaces. May this work lead to healing, holiness, resilience in our diverse community of Jewish women, and beyond.

Rabbanit Dasi Fruchter

Introduction
by Sara Rozner Lawrence

Monologues from the Makom was born from a backdrop of silence. When I was a young girl growing up in the Orthodox Jewish community, sex was not something we talked about. While there were vague references to the shadowy world of "relations," they were always accompanied with warnings and shaming terms so that we would know it was wrong. The well-intentioned educators in my all-girls schools made their best efforts to instill in us both a sense that our bodies were holy and that they were dangerous, a source of inadvertent temptation for men.

When they told us that "boys only want one thing," I felt a stab of fear, not because I was afraid of male aggression, but because I thought I knew what that one thing was and I wanted it too. What did it make me, I wondered, if I as a girl was curious about sex, if I felt flashes of heat and desire when I read the kissing scenes in my novels? What did it make me, I wondered, if I as a girl felt drawn to the other girls, if I sometimes felt that sense of curiosity and arousal during slumber parties? What did it make me, I wondered, if I, as a girl, masturbated? In the absence of any adult acknowledgement of my burgeoning sexuality, I came to my own answer: I must be a freak. Sex was obviously something terribly wrong and inappropriate that only boys had the misfortune to want, I thought. So if I was thinking about it or wanting it or feeling curious about it, I must be both freakish and sacrilegious.

Now as a psychology doctoral student, I've come across numerous studies indicating that abstinence-only sex education is ineffective; merely teaching children to avoid having sex is actually associated with kids beginning to have sex at younger ages, contracting more STDs, and having more unintended teenage pregnancies. For me, though, what these statistics don't capture is the emotional burden that I and many other young people have experienced at the hands of religious abstinence-only sex education. Silence and secrecy about sex breed shame. When something as developmentally central as sexuality is ignored by parents and educators, many children naturally come to the conclusion that there must be something wrong and shameful and embarrassing about it. And that feeling does not always dissipate as people enter adulthood; many young adults in our community are left with a lingering sense of guilt about their sexuality even as they attempt to enter into fulfilling sexual relationships.

As a young woman in college I began to identify and think about this problem, both from an individual perspective and from a communal perspective. To explore the issue from a more academic standpoint, I researched and wrote my thesis about Orthodox women's comfort with sexuality; I conducted a study examining the various factors that contribute to the discomfort with sexuality that I had observed in myself and others throughout my upbringing. On a more personal level, I began a quest to rid myself of the pervasive sense of sexual shame that I felt growing up. Therapy played a large role in that healing process, but I found that almost as powerful as talking about sexual shame in therapy was talking about it with my friends and peers. The more I opened up about it, the more I found I was not alone. Nearly everyone I spoke to shared some element of my experience, whether the shameful sexual messages were conveyed in school or by a parent, peer, music video, or partner. The more I talked to my friends about sex, the more I realized that almost everyone had felt lonely or uncertain because of their sexuality at some point in their lives. Over and over again, I heard people saying that they were unusual or exceptional because "most girls don't watch porn like I do," or "most girls don't masturbate like I do," or "most girls haven't had sex [as much/as young/with as many partners] as I have," or "most girls are shomer negiah and I'm not," or "most girls my age aren't still virgins like I am," or "most girls my age have kissed someone before and I haven't," or "most girls have at least masturbated and I'm too scared to." And on and on. What I came to realize was that the only thing "most girls" had experienced was some type of embarrassment or shame or guilt about themselves as sexual beings. Speaking to my friends about sex had the immensely positive effect of normalizing our experiences and slowly chipping away at the very sense of shame and uncertainty that we were discussing.

By my last semester of Stern College in May 2016, I felt ready to spread this realization to my peers. I had seen *The Vagina Monologues* by Eve Ensler, which is often performed on college campuses, and I wanted to start something similar at my school that would speak to the unique experiences of Orthodox women. I tentatively pitched my idea to a few friends: we would get together and write our own monologues about our experiences as Orthodox women relating to sexuality, gender and body image, and then we would perform them for each other. My friends loved the idea, and together we came up with the title *Monologues from the Makom*. *Makom* is a Hebrew word that literally means place, but is also the common euphemism for vagina throughout the Talmud and rabbinic literature. We wished to reclaim the very word our sages of blessed memory used to sanitize the mention of our sexual organs. These would be our own vagina monologues, inextricably tied to our experiences as Jewish women within an age-old tradition.

It was clear that such an event would not be approved by our religious college, so it became a grassroots effort. One friend had a large apartment in Washington Heights that we could use, one literature professor gave me permission to advertise the event in her classes, and I put out a call for monologues on the private college Facebook group. I was honestly terrified to create the event; I thought that at most 20 people would come and that I would have to beg my friends to share monologues. To my shock, within a couple of days I had more submissions than we could accommodate in one event, and we were officially in business! Better yet, although the event was organized by me and other cisgender Orthodox women, a number of the people who submitted did not identify as Orthodox, or identified as transgender or gender nonbinary[1], which only added to the beautiful diversity of voices in the project.

That first event was magical. Over 60 women crowded into my friend's living room, spilling out into the hallway, eyes shining in the dim light of the overcrowded room. I knew many of them personally, but there were also many I had never met. Women found out about it through the Facebook event I created, but also through word of mouth, as friends told friends about this opportunity—this moment to finally talk about and celebrate our sexuality and identity as Jewish women. At that first event, a total of 17 women performed monologues on topics ranging from nonbinary gender identity to sex education, from mastur-

---

[1] From the inception of the project, we have consciously defined our audience as all those who identify as Jewish women or who identify elsewhere on the gender spectrum and feel that they belong in a female space. Throughout the book, all references to the women who participated in the project should be read with that broader definition.

bation to struggles with body image. And every single woman in attendance celebrated their bravery and openness with claps and snaps and cheers.

The response to the event was incredibly affirming and humbling. At least a dozen women approached me either in person or via text to tell me that they had deeply needed this gathering, that it had spoken to the discomfort and shame that they were still grappling with. An article was written about the event in a Jewish newspaper, and there was an outpouring of messages and comments asking when the next *Monologues* event would be. It quickly became clear that this could not be a one-off event.

Since then, I have organized two more *Monologues from the Makom* events that have reached even more Jewish women. One was sponsored by the Jewish Orthodox Feminist Alliance (JOFA) and took place at the 2017 JOFA conference, and the second was co-sponsored by JOFA and Jewish Queer Youth (JQY) in July 2017. At each event, I was deeply inspired by the courage of each woman who presented, and moved by the ever-growing tapestry of interwoven stories that have been shared.

During one of those events, the idea was proposed to turn *Monologues from the Makom* into a book, to open up the opportunity to share in this experience beyond what we could reach before. Since then, we have been working to compile monologues and poems and stories written by Jewish women on the themes of sexuality, gender, and body image, and how they intersect with Jewish identity. We hope that this book in your hands will capture the same energy and spirit of the live events for an even wider audience.

This project has truly been carried on the shoulders of several incredible women who have put countless hours into organizing and editing this book. Rivka Cohen worked tirelessly to organize and coordinate the logistics of the editing and publishing process, and kept the project moving ahead even amid conflicting busy schedules. Rebecca Zimilover worked with me from the project's inception as an editor, and took the lead on the many minutiae of the editing and reviewing process. Naima Hirsch joined the team as an editor and helped carry the project forward with her enthusiasm and keen literary eye. Sarah Ricklan invested countless hours working as an editor, and was instrumental in staying in touch with the writers and compiling the work into its final form. This book would not have been at all possible without them, and for that I offer them deep gratitude.

Finally, this book would not have been possible without our incredible writers. We have 32 monologues in the book written by courageous women, each of whom has done our community a great service by sharing their story. Some of the writers will be acknowledged by name within the book, while many have chosen to remain anonymous. In the deepest sense, we hope that this anthology captures not only the individual stories of its writers, but also the collective beauty, resilience, and complexity of the broader community of Jewish women. Our hope in compiling these stories is that other Jewish women might read them and feel a little bit less alone, a little bit less shame, a little bit more seen. We hope that this project can play a part in the pursuit to separate sex from shame and stigma in our community.

Sara Rozner Lawrence
September 2019

Subjectivity

Anonymous

I would not be able to pick my vagina out of a lineup

This is the thought that comes to me
After yet another WhatsApp group conversation in which
I am unable to take part
As my oldest friends chat
Vent
Share
Compare
What's best, what's new
Who's done what, and with whom—

Which pill has which side effects
I think was the topic at hand that day
But it could have been anything
Just another harmless conversation that silenced me
And made me realize how much better
My friends know their bodies
Than I know my own
How of course, it's the soul that's important
But it's my body that has me HERE
And I'm living within the walls of a stranger's home

Just as, even before seminary,
Or before, when, at 14, I decided to keep Shabbat

I was always "the frum one"
Because I would stand up in shul to say the Amidah
So too, I was always "the prudish one"
Frigid
The word of choice
That word defined me for my early adolescence
Because, by 18, I had gone no further than kiss a boy

Sigh
But still
I was there
Out there
And I wanted to be
Kissing those boys
It felt good, and it made me feel good
Pretty
Sexy
Wanted
And I know the dream would be
To have that confidence inside me from the start
But some things feel best measured in the eyes of another

Now I am 21
Shomer negiah for three years
And while I am forever, forever, forever grateful
For what further exploration of my Judaism has brought into my
    life
Sometimes
It hits me with a pang
On how much I'm missing out

My friends conduct themselves with ease
They walk lightly, laugh lightly, dance lightly
Join their bodies with another's
Lightly
And not just boys' bodies
They embrace their own
Their bodies and their pleasures and their passion inside
They never apologize
For living, for trying to get the most out of them as possible

And for me, everything is heavy, hard
Knees and elbows and collarbones and stress
Walking carefully to avoid bumping into a boy
Apologizing when I do

And I'm jealous, I am
Not all the time
But it's there
Jealous of their boyfriends and boy-friends and boys whom they
    haven't known long enough to be friends
Of the ease of companionship, of the feel of another's skin
    against one's own
But also because of how well they know their own bodies

Because this isn't really about my relationship with others
Only a little
It's much more about my relationship with me
Soul and body
Content and container

BUT ONE PERSON

With both elements crucial to keeping her going
I have spent so long since I became frum, trying to keep every
    fire inside of me burning
My personality, and my fashion sense, and my humor, and my
    passions
That I forgot about the one under my tongue
The one between my legs

And I know I can't be the only one
Who feels like their religious journey put them in touch with
    their soul in ways never before imagined
But hung up the line on their body

I am.

Anonymous

This body,
I was taught,
Is holy, is sacred, belongs to God.
Keep it covered
To protect my dignity.

This body,
They said,
Could attract their gazes
Could draw unwanted eyes
Could drown in their yearnings.
We must stay holy
Must keep them holy.

When the skirt disappeared with the sleeves
I felt free
Free from smothering confinement,
From their x-ray vision
From that holiness.

So when you told me
We should do it
That it would be good for me, for us
Peeling off those layers was easy.
I was no longer holy, anyway.

So when I told you
That it hurt.
That it hurt.
That it hurt.
And you didn't stop,
I blamed myself
For peeling away my purity
And giving in to lust.

My self, forgotten.
My thoughts floating away with the pain,
Fake smiles, fake strength, fake purity.

This is for
Every time I speak but can't feel
I feel but can't speak
Every time I cry out in painful memory
Every second I spend scared
For every soul who is hiding.
For those who can't speak.

And for me. For me. Shamelessly, for me.

God isn't fluent in perfection
Doesn't speak in the layers you wear
Doesn't blacken our souls
Doesn't disqualify.
God lives in the tears that you cry
In the pain,
Fighting with you.

You are whole
You are beautiful
You are sacred
You are
You are
You are not to blame.

My feet emerging from this ground
I rise and declare to you
I am holy.
I am holy.

I am already holy.

I am.

I have been trying to write this all week

Dani Jacobson

I have been starting and stopping and pausing and trying
Where to even begin?
Words on a page will never be enough for
My relationship with God
Because that's what my dress code is
My beliefs and my values and
The most important relationship in my life
Expressed on my being
Worn on my literal sleeve
There will never be enough pages
Enough letters
But here I go:

When I was 18, I went off on my gap year
And came back ten months later
Different in countless ways
Having laughed
Cried
Screamed
Thought
Changed
Grown—
Everything about the way I see the world shifted
Yet when I came back all everybody else could see
Was that I was dressed differently than before
Only skirts—long ones—and longer sleeves, too

It was all people would ask me about
"So do you only wear skirts now?"
"So is this, like, for real? For always?"
"So are you going to go back to wearing vests again?"
"But don't you just miss jeans?"
As if I had planned the next few years
Of my religious journey ahead
Instead of still figuring out every step as I go
As I still am, I guess
As if how I dressed was the ONLY, the most important
Reflection of how I was feeling inside
Of where I was at, religiously
Which is still an attitude I find everywhere
And still drives me crazy

The truth is, that, of course I miss jeans
I miss all of it
I miss not standing out all the time
I miss not worrying about certain parts of my body showing
But, three years later, I'm still here, skirts and all
Because I love what I've gained more than I miss what I've lost
And this, I guess, is what I'm trying to share with you here
If you'll let me

The magic word is tzniut
And even within the religious community
It's seen as restrictive, repressive, repulsive
As a leader at a religious camp it is the hardest thing to enforce
The dreaded word, the hated outfit checks
Even on our gap year we were told to change
If we broke the rules

I have been trying to write this all week

To many people reading this
The thought of allowing religion to dictate outfit choice
Might be ridiculous
Incomprehensible
Especially when I then call myself a feminist
How can she be?
Where is the feminism, the empowerment, here?
And I get it
Even within Judaism
Tzniut is taught *terribly*
Every time I have to tell a camper to fix her favorite skirt
Without having the time and the setting to teach her why
I wince
Every time the little boys get away with things
That the girls do not
I rage

Because I really, truly believe that tzniut is something beautiful
Its true meaning is hard to define
But it's along the lines of
Hidden
Beneath the surface
Buried
And this is the way that we are told to live our lives:
"When wilful wickedness comes, then comes disgrace;
*But with the modest (**tznuim**), wisdom." (Proverbs 11:2)*
"With what shall I come before the Lord,
bow before the Most High God? [...]
He has told you, man, what is good,
and what the Lord demands of you:
To do justice, and love kindness,

Monologues from the Makom

And to walk discreetly (v'hatznea lekhet)
with your God." (Micah 6:6-8)
These verses have nothing to do with clothing
Or appearances
Or women
They are about wisdom, and justice, and kindness
And walking with God!
Tzniut is humility
The belief, fundamental to Judaism,
That appearances are not everything
That every person, no matter what their image,
Is beautiful by nature
Of being created in the *image of God*
That the true value is on the inside

And somewhere, sometime,
Along the long history of thought, and teaching
Dominated, obviously, by men
This crucial belief of the value being on the inside
Was applied almost exclusively to women
And to what they wear
And that makes me angry
The fact that a concept, such a beautiful, important value
Was turned into a set of rules with which to measure
Skirt lengths and sleeves
With which to teach young girls that they are something to hide
That their bodies are ugly
That even their voices are promiscuous
That they should not be heard, but not seen either

So why do I carry on?

I have been trying to write this all week

Because I still believe in the beauty of the message
Despite it all
I like the statement that my appearance does not define me
The physical expression of how
Very insignificant my physical being is
In relation to my soul
Even now, when I start worrying about looking good
(which I still do, of course)
I catch myself, remind myself
Of what it means, really, to live a tzanua lifestyle
It's not about knees or elbows or what boys might see
It's not about my face, or my hair,
Or being fat, or thin, or in between
It's about quietly, happily, walking with God
And, having chosen to live this way
By myself, for myself
It doesn't feel like oppression, but liberation

I know that may be hard to grasp
But it's true
I love the fact that I can go to any place, in front of anyone
And never worry about being dressed appropriately
The impression that I'm giving
Because it's always the same
There is continuity, genuineness, in that
And
In today's world, obsessed with the physical,
Where more is always more
It's liberating to go against the flow
To say that my body is mine, and not the world's
It feels good to decide not to play the game

I know that my body is not something I have to hide
It's beautiful, and strong, and it carries me
But ultimately, it's just a body
It will crumble and creak and slow down; it's not *me*
Inside
Behind the body
That's where I am
And what's more
Three years, now, since my gap year
I like the statement that what I learned then
Has stayed with me
What I did then remains present
My religion walks with me, on my body
Every step that I take

And I really, truly understand that it's not for everybody
That different things empower different women
Nudity
Modesty
A mix
Either, depending on the day
And nobody should ever tell another which is which
A contradiction, I guess, to the idea of formalized religion
But it's important to separate what should be done from what
has always been done
And to realize that what helps connect one person to God may
not help another
We aren't all the same
We have different challenges, different struggles
I disagree with forcing anybody to do anything that limits them,
that holds them back

But to me, in my own life
I don't think tzniut has done that
It's going to take more than a skirt to dull my shine
If anything, it has done the opposite
Because I am, now, more than ever, what I say and do
I am my personality—I am my soul, all along

So yes
I started keeping the rules of tzniut
Because that's what they were
The rules
But I continued, of my own volition
Because they were so much more

Invisibility

Joy Feinberg

It's Simchat Torah and the rabbi asks if everybody had a chance
   to participate in the service.
He asks just like that, mouth holding each syllable of
Every. Body.
But here in this balcony, in these most sacred moments, I don't
   inhabit a body as I and the women around me participate in
   nothing at all.
Cut off and quarantined, mumbling to ourselves the faint
   prayers that prove we have reason, perhaps, to even show up.

Invisibility in religion falls like a heavy cloak
Until it feels like even God can't see me,
That He's forgotten He created me,
And the body He gave me betrays me every time I come to pray
   with all its femininity.
These days I am a ghost haunting my old temples,
Drifting in and out of services that vaporize me with language
   that cannot fit my tongue.
"He" and "Him" all monopolize my hymns
Until I wonder if I'm praying with someone else's voice
For someone else's rights at someone else's choice;
Like my hands and heart were never built to hold dreams of
   their own.

When you dress the invisible woman
You must do so with care

Cover her brightly glowing skin, knees, elbows and shins,
And when she marries, cover her hair.
Until she is a smothered flame, smoke edging out until there's
    nothing left to see,
Every inch of fabric begging *don't notice me*
I am six—staring at a bus stop sign reminding me
Immodesty is deadly.
I am eighteen—being pulled out of class because a rabbi was
    offended by my knees, my education held hostage at the price
    of his security

When you arm the invisible woman
Give her less and less to hold
Downplay every role that might make her indispensable until
    there is no more to her than a womb
Teach her that her voice is more sacred the less it's put to use
Until she goes mute waiting for words worth saying.
I am twelve—watching my father be honored for my bat mitzvah
My uncle, my grandfather, men that haven't stepped foot in a
    shul in years.
I am thirteen—at a stranger's table watching every mouth
    around me sing out praises to a God offended at my tone,
    holding my tongue in shaking hands,
clearing dishes.

When you teach the invisible woman
Put her in a classroom of her own
Keep books from her hands
Lest she demand what the laws laid out as her due
The glory the prophets promised her—a dancing Miriam, a
    singing Devorah

Lest she try to become the women the Torah called exalted
Until her mind shrinks itself to accommodate the smaller size
   they taught her it should take
I am fifteen—arguing text for text with a boy two years older
   than me when he pulls back to reprimand me:
What am I doing ruining myself
With concepts that don't concern me,
Reading books that weren't written for me,
Memorizing laws that will just distract me?
If I am not careful, no one will want to date me.

What do you do when what you love most of all doesn't fit you?
When the space you call home rejects you?
How do you pour your love over and over into a toxic bank,
Keep shouting for help to a deaf jury—
A room full of lawmakers who will never look anything like you.

I am nineteen—shaking apart in the arms of my favorite teacher
   as she tells me maybe
Orthodoxy isn't the place for me.
How do you leave the only place they taught you it was safe to
   exist?
Where do you go when every fiber of your body wants to wrap
   itself around these balcony guardrails, cement itself to this
   home?
Wants to fall on its knees at the open door of an ark and cry
   until you're forgiven for whatever makes you less-than.
I am four years old—wrapping myself in my father's prayer
   shawl,
Not knowing then that it was as close to a divine embrace as I
   would ever be allowed.

When you kill the invisible woman
Imprint on her tombstone the virtues you bred her for
Make her daughter light candles there
Write songs about her with notes no other invisible woman can
    sing

Until we are all just empty voice boxes on a balcony
And I am just a body-less woman coaxing my own daughter
Back from the edge as she leans over to gaze
At her father and brothers
Teaching her we're better off, up here
In our place.

An Empty Place

Tess

Tal was the first girl I ever had sex with. She was a fast-talking Israeli, the kind that made me shrink back inside myself for fear of saying something that was destined to be wholly misunderstood and irreversible. But she was real and confident and loud and kept saying how much she wanted to kiss me, to touch me. And that's how it happened. In the end she finished and I didn't... what she was doing to my body felt good, but I was missing the usual heat, the chemistry that I usually have with men, or maybe just with my longtime boyfriend. Although maybe she was just too fast, too cool, too smooth to ever let heat simmer thickly between her and a stranger. So maybe it was her; maybe it was me. Or maybe I wasn't really there to lose myself in an eruption of feeling, but rather to feel myself be moved by the shy screaming rhythm of femininity, to be so unashamedly woman, naked and vulnerable and open against my instincts of self-protection. And at age 24, I experienced for the very first time, with my own hands, my own fingers, that the inside of a woman really is hollow, really is aching to be filled with something...sometimes anything. I also learned that hollow doesn't mean dead or dispassionate, but alive and yearning. That emptiness, gasping with the need to be filled, is perhaps the most vital sign of life I can think of.

While, for me at least, there is something wild and true and utterly musical about two bodies fitting together, two warring chemistries learning again and again and again that each one ends where the other begins, there is also something thrilling about two of the same mold swaying with open-mouthed wonder at the majestic beauty of their own self-sufficiency. It feels like the deliciously slippery edge of a spiraling freefall, a drunken revel at the breathtaking power of one's own sex. But as the thrill fades, my feverish conceptualizing thins into tangible shapes and I contemplate Tal...her fast-paced confidence, how she told me that for her a good party can be even better than sex, her failed relationships, her awkward attempts at intimacy, and her fear of jellyfish and death that she confessed to me without any illusion of context as we sat naked and wrapped in a salt-sticky sheet, velvety ocean breeze blowing through our damp hair, her smoking a third cigarette and me wondering when it was appropriate to start making moves to head home. I thought of how someone could be so much, and so much of the right things, but still not enough, or maybe just not enough of the true thing.

She drove me home, and before I left her sandy and barefoot in her car, I kissed her lips lightly and let myself hover in her space for a beat. My first true act of initiation the whole night. She smiled without speaking, her first true act of reception. And I thought about parting, and how lips part and legs part and people part, and how an opening is both a beginning and an end, and we both overuse and underuse our power to dictate where things should start and where they should finish and when they are full and how they should be filled. And how the world isn't comfortable with allowing the hollow spaces of the world to speak of their emptiness. And how women carry around hollow spaces in their own bodies that make the world so uncomfortable when all they have to do is accept the fact that the non-binary patterns of human life leave spaces that we don't know how to fill. And that each imperfect, temporary attempt is a creation of beauty in itself. And even though it is never perfect or enough, it is, at the same time, both.

Lucy, I Love You

Panmi

What I most recall was the all-consuming, ravenous hunger that fell upon me when the nausea of early pregnancy passed. My desire for food came rushing back, and with it, an onslaught of every other kind of craving imaginable. It was as if I had returned to the land of the living. I had a round belly with an unborn child kicking and playing in the primordial waters that sustained it, and my hormones were juicing me up with a lubricating and passionate appetite.

But I wasn't just hit with a physical hunger. My libido suddenly returned from the dead. It consumed my every waking moment. I wanted sex. And more specifically, I wanted women.

It was the first time in my life that the inchoate mess of suppressed longing, lifelong curiosity, attraction and displacement came together in a perfect storm. This was an incomprehensible and irrepressible need for whatever I could imagine as a sexual encounter with a member of the fairer sex.

I whispered my fantasies to my husband at night. He tried with his body and all of his imagination to ease the cravings, but it wasn't enough.

I guess he really did love me, because ultimately he braved the adult video shop with me. Though I had passed the shop many times, a lifetime of devout religious upbringing left its forbidden charms a complete stranger to me. Only desperation fed my newfound bravado. For the first time, I walked right up and did not hustle past with eyes shielded and face turned toward the ground.

We went into the shop together—he with his long side locks and velvet yarmulka and I with my eight-month pregnant belly, headscarf, and sensible shoes. The gentleman at the counter asked if we were in the right place, and then asked what I preferred in my pornographic material. I mumbled something about women, my face flushed and terrified of being found in this place.

I got *Lucy, I Love You*, a compilation of half-hearted girl-on-girl action. But more than the porn itself, I got Lucy, a beautiful redhead whose brazenly bared surgically enhanced breasts were my first foray into naming and addressing the longing of my heart and mind. I had Lucy and my fingers and the almost incessant waking dreams that colored the afternoons where I allowed my mind to wander back to Lucy and her glorious body.

Many years later, I am here. I am in the strange no man's land between admitting my queerness with flying colors, and suppressing and guarding the portals to my passion. I live this way, never fully belonging anywhere because respectable, devoutly religious, husband-loving, pious and passionate, careful and responsible Jews don't get to taste a woman and live to tell about it.

I am this way because loving women is a deep and dark secret that has the power to ruin and destroy so many lives. The lives of my husband and my children. I cannot acknowledge the basic and simple joy, the beautiful life-affirming pleasure of exchanging sexual caresses with my female lovers because to do that would be instant social death.

Eighteen forever years ago, I gave a space to those emerging feelings, and fed them with images on my video screen. How my life could be now if I acted on my feelings! If I kiss a woman on her mouth, and propel my fantasy into life. Could it be that all of those years melt into nothingness, all of the yearning faded away… And could it be more gratifying and more fulfilling than I ever imagined so many years ago?

I am this way because of Lucy. Because I am unable to recall a time before her, before being with a *her* meant everything in the world to me. That is why I am here before you today.

And this is my story.

The Girl Who Loved Masturbating/ My Complicated Relationship with Masturbation

Shainy

I was nine years old when I had my first orgasm. I was in the bath, and the experience was so pleasurable that as I climaxed I watched the color of the wall tile become more vivid and beautiful. Confused about what had happened, I told my mother about it; she gave me a strange look, and insinuated that it wasn't something I should ever do again.

I did it again anyway.

I just didn't tell her about it.

Masturbation and sexual fantasy came so naturally to me. It was my guilty pleasure. The guilt always accompanied the pleasure.

Despite my mother's discouragement, every night in the darkness of my room and in the hushed silence before sleep, I'd slip my hand between my legs and begin to daydream. I learned quickly to have silent orgasms. And to hate creaky beds. And quickly began to hate myself for having dirty thoughts.

I was a top student in school. Because of that, I was given permission to use the school library after finishing my work. There, alone, I looked up "sexual intercourse" in the *Encyclopedia Britannica*. I discovered the word masturbation, and learned that my nighttime pleasures were a normal experience, and that the associated guilty feelings were regrettably common. Still, I remained convinced that I was the only frum girl who did it.

As I grew older, I felt increasingly annoyed with myself. Without anyone telling me so, I had come to the "obvious" conclusion that sexuality was the antithesis of tzniut. I was becoming more serious about my frumkeit and was convinced that I needed to stop masturbating. An entry in my diary reveals my "NMEA" Project ("Never Masturbate Ever Again!"). There are two paltry checkmarks on a chart that was supposed to have documented at least a week without masturbating. I couldn't help it. It felt too good to give up. And so I hated myself for my lack of resolve.

Other than being a masturbation fanatic, I was a very good frum girl. I dressed in a tzanua way. I wore only tights, not socks. I threw out a sweater when I was 13 because it emphasized my chest. I didn't wear pants until I was 15 years old. My wardrobe was basically black with the occasional colored top. I wonder now if I was overcompensating for feeling too sexual.

In high school we learned about zera l'vatala. That male masturbation wasted sperm. I understood what was wrong there, but the reason for females not to masturbate was a little more vague. Something about… saving pleasure to have with our husbands? Yeah, well. Too late for that, anyway. And so I hated myself for being beyond redemption.

In my early twenties I got married and could finally feel less guilty about my sexuality. The permissibility of sex was a huge relief. My kallah teacher liked to stress that it was a mitzvah to have sex, and I got the impression that she dealt with many kallahs who were too stressed to experience sexual pleasure, or had too limited an understanding of their bodies to do so. I was immensely grateful that sex was a pleasurable experience for me, and I know that my fantasies have greatly contributed to a wonderful sex life!

As a parent, I have already given my young children more of a sex education than I ever had. I aim to help them understand that sex and sexuality are an integral part of our humanity, and don't exist in a vacuum. I hope that they can lead healthy sexual lives without any emotional baggage. As I teach them, I've been educating myself and forgiving the young girl who liked to touch herself in bed at night, and the teenager with the healthy sex drive.

These days, I'm a busy mother, employee and university student. But I still make some "special time" for myself.

Only these days I'm calling it self-love.

It's Different Than the Movies

Rebecca Krevat

Everything I knew about sex I learned from movies. I knew
I wanted a boyfriend. I knew I wanted to be kissed. I imagined
it happening at the top of grand staircase like Cher and Josh in
Clueless, or during detention like in *The Breakfast Club*, or in a
flying car like at the end of *Grease*. I had no idea what any of
that meant, though, or how I could make it happen for myself. I
had crushes as a young girl, but little came of them. I used to sit
in the grass on our lag ba'omer trips and watch the lanky boys
of my high school run with their skinny legs and sneakers that
all seemed to be two sizes too big. The one thing I knew is that
I wanted my first kiss to be with a boyfriend—I wanted it to
feel important, special. My friends talked about boys in a very
dreamy, abstract way too. None of us had the romantic encoun-
ters that I was seeking.

When I was 13 a friend I had a crush on touched my thigh
when I didn't want him to. We were sitting in the movies, and
some of our other friends were there. I shifted and twisted my
body until I was barely sitting on the chair anymore; I was halfway up the armrest. I couldn't say "no" or "stop that" because I
didn't want my friends to hear. I couldn't say anything because
part of me was also excited. I had a crush on him, and here he
was—trying to touch me. I couldn't say anything, and it felt like
when you want to scream during a nightmare but can't. I could
not place this kind of interaction in the movies I watched. Mark
Darcy didn't secretly try to touch Bridget Jones when no one was
looking; he kissed her purposefully, out in the snow, with deep

feeling. When it was finally over we walked towards the bathroom together. I remember looking down at the dark red carpet, worn thoroughly by too many footsteps, avoiding his gaze. When he asked me to keep it to myself, I said that I would. I knew in a dark place that he wasn't touching me because he liked me.

Time went on, and I graduated from the eighth grade. I had my first kiss at summer camp, on Shabbat afternoon sitting outside on the grass. We both had braces. We were chewing fruit flavored gum. He was a sweet boy who asked me later in the summer if he could unhook my bra. Thrilled at the question even being asked, I said no quickly and quietly. I didn't know what I wanted, but he listened to me. We spent the rest of the summer making out everywhere.

More experience apparently meant that I was more vulnerable to further intrusions and confusing unwanted attention. The boy who touched my legs when I didn't want him to, who I thought was my friend, started writing to me online. Asking me questions.

"Have you had your first kiss yet?"

"Did he touch you anywhere else?"

"Do you touch yourself in bed at night?"

"Did you and your friends shower together at camp?"

I would see him in the hallways at school, and sometimes he was so friendly I wondered if maybe he did like me as more than a friend. I liked him too. I didn't like the questions he would ask me online, though. They made me feel embarrassed, too ashamed to even tell my friends. Still, I kept talking to him. I didn't know what else to do. I liked him and wasn't sure how to express myself, to change the situation, to find out what was going on underneath. Did he want to be my boyfriend but wasn't sure how to tell me yet? It seemed to me like a classic romantic comedy plot—boy can't figure out how to tell girl he likes her, so instead he chats her online until he eventually does.

One night he invited me over to his parents' house. I could barely shut the door before he grabbed me and started kissing me. It was exciting, exhilarating, dangerous. He took out his penis. I had never seen one before.

"You can touch it if you want."

"Um, hm, I don't know."

"It's okay."

"I really don't know."

"Here."

He grabbed my hand and put it on his penis.

"Here. Like this."

He moved my hand up and down.

I started thinking about if this is what it was supposed to feel like. I thought about the movies, and couldn't remember seeing any of these feelings reflected back from the glittering smiles of young girls and women falling for the boys and men of their dreams. Maybe these are the parts that are edited out in the TV versions.

"Put your mouth on it."

And so he ordered me to give my first blow job. He put his hand on the back of my head and roughly pushed my head back and forth until I had tears in my eyes. I didn't ask him to stop. I didn't know what I was doing or why I was doing it but I kept thinking about the movies. When Kat Stratford and Patrick Verona are falling in love during *10 Things I Hate About You*, there was way more laughter. After he came, he offered me a Sprite because he could tell I was surprised at how gross his semen tasted. I took a sip and I left.

Meetings like these continued, following the same set of rules. He would tell me where to meet him, and I would oblige. The hidden bathroom upstairs at my shul. Cabs home from school. He would tell me what to do and I would submit like a pet. "Sit, stay—kiss me here, touch me there. Good girl." Never once did he ask me if I wanted to be doing this. If there was anything I wanted. If there was anything that would make me feel good.

There were times that I tried to say no. When he would send me pictures of his penis. When he would ask to meet up. When he would call me to masturbate over the phone. I tried to say no. He always found a way to coerce me into complying. It was easier to just do whatever he wanted and get it over with than to keep on fighting with him.

I felt like I was in a windowless room. I was alone, and scratching at the cement walls would only have bloodied my fingers. I finally met a different boy who became my boyfriend, and suddenly, somehow, my no meant something. I finally had a legitimate reason for rejecting him.

I didn't learn the word consent until college. The sex education at my Modern Orthodox day school was spotty and unmemorable. If students were having good experiences touching each other it was because of their own respect and care for each other. It wasn't because they were given the tools and empowered with possibilities by the people who were supposed to teach us how to be good humans in this world. I wish my high school feared less about students having sex, and more about students being abused. I wish I was taught a language for how to deal with any of it, not just lines that sounded sweet in fictional characters' mouths. Growing up I learned not to talk to strangers, and to stay where I was if I ever got lost, how to study for exams, when to bow during prayers. I was never taught how to respond when the real villains were people who were supposed to be my friends, or how sex is supposed to be pleasurable, or how women are not just vessels and holes and hands for men.

I held this secret of my youth so tightly that I had panic attacks, sometimes so severe I couldn't go to class. It wasn't until college, when I went to therapy for the attacks, that the dots of what happened to me were connected and I could finally start to heal. The confusing feelings that plagued me as a young teen, the emotions memorialized only in diaries like amateur scripts that never saw the light of day, that I threw out because they contained so many pages of written shame, all of that was unearthed until I could be free. I continue carrying this baggage to every relationship I enter, heavy like a film's plot conflict, but at least now I'm the protagonist and not a passive extra whose scene lies on the cutting room floor. I wield the pen, and it's my story to tell. I don't quite feel like a hero, but at least I'm finally in control of the narrative.

You didn't prepare for me?

I had recently stopped identifying as shomer negiah and I was
  confused about what I wanted.

He was sure what he wanted.

It was our fourth date, our second time making out. He asked if
  we could do more.

I said I wasn't sure.

He asked again.

And again.

And again.

Until I gave in.

When he put his hand down my pants and felt my never-shaven
  vagina, he asked, "You didn't prepare for me?"

Never mind that I did my hair and makeup.

Never mind that I wore my sexiest dress.

Never mind that I planned out the entire day's activities.

Never mind that I **had** prepared for him.

But my pubic hair? No, I hadn't prepared that for him.

I hadn't prepared, I wasn't prepared.

I was pressured, not prepared.

Shame

Anonymous

I knew in my gut it was wrong. He kept texting me, sweet-talking me, sending me lists of all the reasons why we should hook up again. I kept saying no but I realized I wasn't getting through to him. I even gave my phone to a friend to intervene on my behalf, and he finally relented, saying he would just come visit me as a friend.

I had been going to this Orthodox sleepaway camp for 8 years and it felt like my home away from home. This guy and I had worked together at camp the summer before and had spent a few weeks hooking up. I didn't want to hook up with him again, and I definitely didn't want him to come to camp expecting that, so I told him how I felt. He assured me he just wanted to hang out as friends and had no ulterior motive.

He sexually assaulted me during his visit.

I thought about telling the camp I had been assaulted, but I was worried that that would mean explaining that we had hooked up the summer before. I did not want to get kicked out of camp for touching a member of the opposite sex, which was against camp policy. The camp had kicked people out in the past for doing that very thing, and I was worried I would be the next person forced off campus if I came forward. At least that's the lie I told myself. I couldn't believe the assault happened, and I didn't think anyone else would believe me either.

Even worse, my parents worked at the camp and I knew that if I came forward my parents would definitely find out. We had never discussed sex, and talking about a sexual assault would

Monologues from the Makom

have been horribly uncomfortable. I knew we wouldn't be able to communicate in a way that would have made me feel better. To this day my family still does not know.

It's been over five years since the assault and three years since I began going to therapy. Even after all of this time, I am still struggling with the reality of what happened. It took me two years after the assault happened to tell someone in an authoritative position. At that point I was working as a dorm counselor, and as part of our training during orientation week we had to take a sexual assault course. Sitting in a room full of people discussing how to best handle a student who reports an incident of sexual assault was my breaking point. I wasn't able to sit through the course, and it was at that point that I realized I needed to seek help.

I finally got the courage to approach the school counselor; I told her I had been sexually assaulted two years prior and needed a therapist to talk to since I had never processed what had happened to me. She recommended I reach out to a program called the Takanot Project which helps Orthodox men and women who have been sexually assaulted. Without that program I can't even imagine how lost I would be today. The therapist I saw worked with me on the shame I felt over my relationship history with my assailant. I worked on forgiving myself for ignoring the signs and for letting us explore our sexuality together the year before. It was hard to differentiate whether I truly thought he was a bad guy or if the fault lay with me for being sexual with him; if I hadn't, I thought, maybe he would never have assaulted me. I'm still working on not blaming myself for my assault and recognizing that nothing gave him the right to force himself on me the way he did.

I realize now that I didn't go against my upbringing by being sexually assaulted. For a long time shame, embarrassment, and guilt plagued me every time I thought about the assault or about touching a member of the opposite sex. Unhealthy thoughts plagued me for two years, like *I was wearing a short skirt when he came to visit me that Sunday; did the assault happen because I was wearing a short skirt? Did the assault happen since I let him touch me before? Maybe Orthodoxy is right and I should not be intimate with members of the opposite sex because this is what happens.* I am so grateful that I sought treatment for these cognitive distortions, since these thoughts prevented me from being able to have a healthy relationship. I was taught that hooking up with men is wrong and shameful and had to re-learn how to be healthy and intimate with a man I love. I was petrified to touch a guy since I was scared it would lead to him assaulting me; my brain unfortunately made that automatic connection.

When I started shidduch dating and was dating men who were shomer negiah, all I could think about on the first few dates was, *If I don't give this man an opportunity to touch me, how will I know he won't sexually assault me on our wedding night, once we are finally allowed to touch?* Therapy helped me tremendously but my experience that summer has unfortunately left permanent damage. Now I only date men who are not shomer negiah so that I will have time to trust them physically before marriage. I unfortunately get asked by some "well-meaning" friends how I can be intimate with a man before marriage and not feel guilty. This question feels like a slap in the face. I didn't ask for this baggage.

I wish somewhere in my upbringing someone had explained consent to me or had taken the time to say, "If you plan on touching a man outside of marriage, here is what you should know." Instead, my community did not discuss these things and

I was forced to learn about it in therapy, once it was already too late. When I reached out to my mentors in high school, I was told there was no such thing as platonic friendships with guys; our school used to show us videos and studies that proved men and women cannot be just friends. Growing up in an environment that felt this way toward friendships made me feel that I did not have the language or tools at my disposal to talk to anyone about sexual relationships with men. I wish I had learned what a healthy relationship involving touch looked like instead of having to navigate it on my own.

Consent

Joy Feinberg

Here
in the shivering moonlight
sinew and bone begging to retreat
my mouth begins a desperate quest to bite through its own
    tongue
anoint itself with its own blood
distill something holy from the tremors, the ink stains,
the humble way my hand wants to touch back and can't—
    restrained by growing words—
and so hovers still, somewhere close enough to feel the heat of
    skin

growing words to plant a young girl in
to till the soil of her imaging of herself
they promise:
A diamond is most safe when it remains under key,
Candy most desired when it is still in the wrapper
no one wants an apple with a bite missing—
woman and her wants repurposed in metaphors
girl made object with the best-by date stamped in black ink
    across her arm
splitting herself open into the hands of a man like she was hers
    to give away.

Sex-ed is a foreign term
A universe I cannot conceive of

Listen to my friends talk about condoms on bananas like I am
    an anthropologist
Like we didn't go to schools two blocks from each other.
Where I was taught to make an altar of my body, an offering to
    whatever left me still whole
still something worthy of love
The first time we kissed, I cried in that unmade bed for an hour
asked—how can I ever love you enough to pour out my body
    against the blunt of these horns

sometimes,
I watch couples in cafes, in restaurants
watch them hold each other in a desperate bid to re-educate
    myself
hours devoted to unlearning the stepping stones sewn into my
    earliest lessons.
This is not finding out you've been mispronouncing a word
This is discovering you learned the alphabet wrong
and every sentence you've ever spoken before this moment was
    nonsense. Unreadable.
All you are is fluent in a language that was never real

But this, they tell me,
this is how you break brainwashing—it hurts every single time
    until it doesn't.

when I close my eyes, my body is finite
it is a countable number of pieces I give away, in mouths and
    hands
until I am left with nothing
it has never belonged to me

When I dream, I am dressed in shrink-wrap
covered in translucent, it clings to my skin
traps all of my pieces together in one place, keeps me from
    shattering apart
I cannot lose any of myself
I am loved through the plastic
If you hold me, it is like we are not even really touching

See Me

Michelle Alya

Look!
Look at me!
What do you see?

Do you see a female gender?
Do you see an overweight body type?
Do you see the creases created by my expressions of love, compassion, laughter, sadness, pain, powerlessness, longing, or hopelessness?
Do you see what is beneath? What's inside? The truth? The integrity? What's real?

You probably don't. It's not something I show willingly. It's not something I let anyone see.

Growing up, to have a feeling meant to cover up that feeling. To have a thought meant to be quiet. To have a question meant to not ever be answered.

Look!
Look at me!
What do you see?

Do you see a woman who has been beaten countless times by her parents in her youth?
Do you see a woman who was raped at the age of 8 and 16?

Do you see a woman who has struggled with burning her flesh and cutting her core in order to feel real?
Do you see a woman who has starved herself to look like an image portrayed as perfection?

You probably don't. It's not something I show willingly. It's not something I let anyone see.

In high school when I was raped for the second time, I was told that it was my fault. How I looked. How I dressed. Every external part of my being was why I was to blame. It didn't matter that deep within I did not want this. It didn't matter that deep within, a warrior was chained up and muzzled not to speak! It didn't matter that my soul was yelling, screaming, crying to come out and reclaim me. Reclaim myself! It just didn't matter.

Look!
Look at me!
What do you see?

Do you see a woman who had her life taken away?
Do you see a woman who had her youth stolen?
Do you see a woman who was told to keep quiet?
Do you see a woman who was told not to feel?

You probably don't. It's not something I show willingly. It's not something I let anyone see.

You Shouldn't Have

Anonymous

Inspired to write while pondering Yom Kippur and forgiveness. Inspired to publish while pondering the "Me too" campaign and resistance.

I wish I had the guts to say this to your face:

You should have asked before you put your arm around my shoulder, when I said I hadn't known it was a date. You should have asked before you slid your hands around my waist. You should have asked before you kissed my stiff, unsure, uncomfortable neck. You should have asked before you put your hands in my bra.

You should have known not to put the tips of your fingers on the small of my back, just because I passed by. And you damn well should have known not to grab my butt as you passed me in the street, laughing.

You shouldn't have complimented my hair, my forearms, or my butt. You shouldn't have yelled at me in French, Spanish, Arabic, Hebrew, or English. You shouldn't have flicked a rubber band at me from a moving car. You shouldn't have made hissing cat noises or asked me explicitly to have sex with you as I waited to cross the street.

You shouldn't have said, "You're too pretty to cry," when I couldn't find my travel buddy, when I was alone in a foreign country, and when you were trying to lure me back to your apartment.

You shouldn't have tried to kiss me after abandoning me in said foreign country when I eventually returned to the hostel, distraught, and told you what had transpired.

You shouldn't have said, "I want you to get me off...when you're ready," after an agonizingly silent car ride in which you yelled at me that nothing was bothering you...and when you knew I wasn't nearly ready. You shouldn't have gotten even more angry when I told you I was trying very hard not to feel pressured.

You shouldn't have angrily hit my hand, however lightly or symbolically, for bringing up that I worried that our relationship was getting too physical.

You shouldn't have said, "If you really loved me, you would," or, "We're not done here," as I tried to pull your hand away, or, "I think you're okay with this," when I said I wasn't sure, or "If it feels good, just let it happen."

It didn't matter if I was wearing pants, a maxi skirt, or a mini skirt. It didn't matter if I was in a club, a bar, the streets, or my own home.

It's been exactly two years since I stopped being shomer negiah. This is part of what I have to show for it. I still feel the need to tell men that it was a recent change, in the hopes that they'll be more considerate. I still question the decision constantly, because of other people's actions. But I shouldn't have to stave off touching men in order to receive physical respect. I shouldn't have to be shomer negiah to get respect, and I shouldn't have to not be shomer negiah to get respect, either. Besides, some of these things happened—and continue to happen—whether I'm shomer or not.

I shouldn't have had to experience these things. And I shouldn't have to grapple with my own emotional self-preservation and the guilt of not calling you out for the sake of the feminist cause. I shouldn't have to call you out and I shouldn't have to tell you what you did was wrong.

These are just some specific examples from multiple men I've encountered in my own life, but I know that many women, men, and non-binary people have experienced similar or much worse. We shouldn't have to endure this and we shouldn't have to tell you that.

You just shouldn't have done it.

You should know better.

Do better.

Welcome to Womanhood

Lucy Benjamin

Before I understood the power I had hidden between my legs, it
  already had a name.
Yiddish sounding: *Shmuggle*, my mother called it.
A young Jewish girl, expected to "be fruitful and multiply;"
I had fallen into a trap through no choice or realization of my
  own.
My femininity and my Jewish identity were entangled,
the chains between the two would soon grow.
A "chained woman" I would become.

At 11, the red stains declared me to be grown.
At 12, my religion did.
The crimson clots named me "woman;"
My religion named them "dirty."
My body put me behind bars in synagogue,
But at least I'll have time for the children, right?

No.

At 18, the monthly pain became too strong,
The screams from the bathroom floor too loud,
The putrid smell of sick too great.

So the periods had to stop—What made me "adult" and
  "feminine" gone.
So what am I now?

Monologues from the Makom

And who are they to say?

At least I am no longer deemed unclean each month.

Built-up Bravery

Jordyn Kaufman

When I was 11, my mom left a package of pads in my bathroom. I didn't have my period yet, so I was a little thrown off. Later, while she stood cooking at the stove, I almost didn't hear her as she sheepishly said, with her back to me, "They're for when you need them." I assumed she was speaking to me because I was the only one in the room, but it was hard to tell over the sound of the sizzling hamburgers. But I was too embarrassed to clarify, and she was too embarrassed to say it more clearly. I went to my bathroom and stowed them away in a place where I would not have to look at them.

But then came the day in eighth grade, sitting in class, when I felt something funky. I went to the bathroom, where I spent three minutes that felt like 30 sitting on the toilet, staring at the piece of bloody toilet paper in my hand, completely baffled and scared. Finally, I wadded up some toilet paper and zipped my purple denim shorts back up. *I'll have to make a doctor's appointment when I get home*, I thought, because that's what you do when you start randomly bleeding.

It seems obvious to me as an adult that if it quacks like a duck and looks like a duck, then...

But when you're 13 and you see blood, even though you've been told in health class about your ever-changing body, the thought just doesn't occur to you. But sitting on the bus and halfway home, I realized—of course it was my period.

When I got home, I went to my bathroom to retrieve the forgotten pads. I read the instructions, and gingerly stripped away the wrapping and protective sheets before placing it on a clean pair of underwear. For the next three months, I used this two-year old secret stash, and didn't tell anyone I had gotten my period.

Then my worst nightmare arrived. I was down to my last few pads. As a young teenager with no money or driver's license, I realized I would have to confess to my mother that I was now "a woman." Instead of finally talking to her about it, I took the now-empty plastic package from the pads, and left it on my mom's dresser while she slept.

When I got home from school that day I found that mom had gone to the store, picked up some more, and left them in my bathroom. No words spoken about it. We went through this silent ritual several more times, until one day when she texted me: "Do you like this kind?" To which I replied, "I guess?" And that was that.

My body became a taboo topic that I couldn't talk about. I couldn't face my mom to talk about all that I was experiencing.

Six months later, I started to experience what was (at the time) unimaginable pain. Instead of telling my mom or doctor, I googled it and saw that "cramps" were normal. And so I assumed that two days out of every month, when I couldn't get out of bed without the stabbing feeling of 3,000 dull knives running through my lower abdomen, back, and skull, were normal.

I said nothing as the pain overcame my body and washed away every ounce of my will to live. I said nothing as the pain nearly caused me to pass out, taking away my breath every time I tried to stand up. I pretended it was normal so I wouldn't have to talk to anyone about the fact that I was now regularly bleeding out of my vagina.

I became accustomed to taking my comforter, pillow, and water bottle into my bathroom and sleeping on the floor, as lessening any movement helped to slightly ease my pain. But this is normal, I told myself. I'm just like all other girls who also don't talk about it. I'm not sexually active, so I don't need to go to the gynecologist.

I went on like this—living with debilitating pain—until I was 21 years old. But at 21, I had an epiphany. I hopped out of bed and said to my reflection in the mirror, *I owe it to myself to go see a doctor because I'm a feminist who shouldn't be afraid of her vagina.*

I read some reviews of gynecologists online and chose one in the perfect location—right across from Bath and Body Works. Despite good reviews, I realized quickly that I had stepped into the doctor's office from hell. The receptionists and nurses dismissed my concerns and fears. The doctor touched me—an openly terrified young woman—with no warning or permission. She stuck her finger inside me, shocking me in my terrified state.

She offered me a prescription for birth control, but then actually wrote a prescription for the wrong medication. When I went to pick it up, half crying and shaken by my experience in her office, I ended up fighting with my insurance company. I finally managed to get the right prescription, a birth control pill that changed my life.

No more stabbing or nausea. No more sleeping on the floor and not being able to stand. This pill that terrified me—the pill that was so stigmatized in my world—helped create a world free of pain for me.

I had been wallowing over the Mr. Hyde doctor experience for about a week when I made a decision. I would not let my mother's conditioning, or society's decided taboos, or one horrible doctor, stop me from taking care of myself. About a year later I went to my second ever gynecologist appointment. The receptionist and nurses were warm and relieved me of all concerns and the doctor was one of the kindest people I've ever met. She listened to me and made me feel heard before explaining to me every single movement she was going to make. "I'm going to touch your thigh, okay?" she said, and my fear melted away. When it was over, she told me how brave I had been. I laughed and shrugged it off, because it seemed cheesy and overstated, but as I was walking out, that statement held in suspension in my mind. It meant something to me. There shouldn't be a need for bravery at an annual checkup, but after my conditioning and negative experiences, it meant something to me. I had been brave.

I decided I could continue being brave. A week after my revolutionary appointment, I was in my childhood home. The home where I first got my period. The home where I would leave my mother empty packages of pads. The home where I slept on the bathroom floor. The home where the foundation of my femininity was built. But I needed to bring my newfound comfort and awareness to this place. And when I was home, I got my period. I nostalgically checked my bathroom and found an (almost) empty package of pads. I grabbed it and went into the kitchen, where my mother was cooking.

"Mom," I said. She turned around and saw me holding up the plastic. She paused for a moment before a smile curled across her face and she said, "Do you need more pads?" "Yes mom, I do," I said matter-of-factly. "Well, there are more in your little sister's room, so feel free to go and take what you need." And just like that I walked out of the kitchen, laughing to myself about the almost 10 years it took to muster up the courage to see my mother's face as she looked at a torn, empty, plastic bag.

First Period

Jennifer Strauss

Is that…? No. It can't be. Suddenly, the tiniest dark spot in my underwear casts my brain into a frenzy.

I mean, they said this might happen. They never gave me an exact timeline, though, and after so long, I guess I stopped expecting it. I don't think I own any pads. I need to buy pads. I need to tell someone. Should I tell someone? Is this something I'm telling people?

Well, right now, in this restroom, I should probably think of a more immediate next step. I shove a wad of toilet paper into my underpants, flush and wash my hands, and return to my desk at my college internship.

I try to focus on the Word document on the desktop screen and position my fingers on the keyboard, but all I can think is, "Period. Period. I have a period."

It's so strange. I mean, who has a first period when they're already in their twenties? I want to think of it as a new beginning. A resurrection. The "Second Coming," if you will, after years of eating-disorder-induced amenorrhea put my cycle to rest.

No more pretending to commiserate with others about cramps and PMS, summoning remnants of distant memories. No more whispering the answer when asked, "When did you last menstruate?" before routine visits at the university health clinic. No more wanting to die of embarrassment when the radiologist refuses to believe that my doctor prescribed a bone density scan because of my hormone levels. Those are for postmenopausal women, not 20-year-olds. No more nervous breakdowns in the library at 2:00 am over a doctor's email saying the results mean my bones could easily shatter if my estradiol levels don't recover.

"Mazal tov. You can have babies!" That mortifying reaction when I asked for pads at age 12. It's probably why the terrible explanation I've vocalized for not dating between recovery and now was, "Well, I still can't have babies, so..." Who knew periods held my skeleton together?

Maybe now I'll concentrate on studying. Maybe I'll think about having a social life. I'll finally end those thoughts about how not normal I am and how unlike my friends I turned out. Maybe I'll *want* to date. Maybe I'll *want*...I'll want...

Oh, no. This again. No. Uninvited, the thought rushes back to me as swiftly as this flow will to my underwear if the toilet paper doesn't hold up. I'm not prepared to take it back. Not now. After everything. It's louder now. *You. Are. Gay.*

Look, it's not like I forgot I was gay. I've been stuck in a romanceless, sexless rabbit hole, but it's not something you forget. You don't forget peer rumors muttered in disgust at age 13. Or being called "lezzie" in high school hallways before you're even sure of yourself. You don't forget seeking coming out advice on *Buffy the Vampire Slayer* fanfiction message boards because 17-year-old you doesn't know out queer people offline. You don't forget the trembling. The loneliness. Or the beauty. The hope, even.

But when I lost the ability to feel, after time, I doubted those hidden feelings ever existed. It's like someone clamped the faucet to those desires, dumped clear water out, and replaced it with a slimy, brown muck of eating disorder mess. Rendered irrelevant, all the ambitions and confusion that once consumed me in secret sat submerged in an identity-swallowing substance I don't speak of now. Menstrual blood is pristine by comparison.

Ugh. I hate it. Not what I went through, not what I am, but holding on to the secrets and the lies. If I'm going to take control, I need to take ownership of all of it. I'm tired of making vague references to everything I've been too afraid and too ashamed to mention. What point is there to ensuring my bones are intact if I'm still going to walk around presenting fragments of a person?

This certainly isn't about "babies." It doesn't mean I can get back everything I lost, medically or otherwise. I know I can't. I don't need to be what I was before to be whole. So, I'll start here, after my second first period, my second time discovering sex, my second time coming to terms with being a lesbian. My body and adulthood, take two. Here I go.

Oy, to Be a Tomboy

Ellen Levitt

At the age of five I was not listening to all of the typical 1960s messages about gender norms. Though I liked to play with nail polish like many girls my age, I was also telling people that when I grew up, I wanted to play baseball for the New York Mets.

Fast forward to the present day, at age 55. I have given up on my youthful dream of playing professional baseball. I only occasionally paint my nails. But throughout my life I have had people question some of my interests, activities and actions because they did not seem "feminine" enough. As a child, I had an uneasy feeling about being dubbed a tomboy. I was one of those kids who just wanted to do what interested me, without it being categorized as feminine or masculine. I joined the Girl Scouts and liked to wear skirts sometimes. I enjoyed collecting stuffed animals, interior decorating, and baking, all activities which were perceived as girlish. But I also liked sports (especially baseball), I was interested in technology and silent movies, and I wanted to learn how to chant Torah. Some people chuckled at this, or raised their eyebrows, or rolled their eyes. I picked up on their attitudes but tried not to feel too self-conscious about my choices. Even as an adult, I have a bit of self-consciousness regarding certain activities and choices I make, which I tend to hide behind bravado or shrugs. I purposely tell myself not to let the questions irritate me.

I distinctly recall one Erev Simchat Torah at the East Midwood Jewish Center when I was 12 or 13. The entire congregation was dancing in the street, and at some point an adult handed me a Torah to dance with. I was excited and felt grown-up that someone trusted me with a Torah, so I grasped it carefully and began to march around. But then another man grabbed it away from me and told me I couldn't dance with the Torah. I was angry. Was it because I was a girl? Or did he think I was too young or too weak to handle the Torah? Did he think it looked bad for a girl to be seen in public with a Torah? I do not know.

Surprisingly, another sphere in my life which was male-dominated was my teaching. For 20 years I taught social studies at the high school and middle school levels. With the exception of one school, there were always more male than female teachers in the social studies department, and I never taught under a female assistant principal. On the surface, history and social studies classes don't seem inherently more masculine or more likely to be taught by men, but in reality there were always more men teaching these classes than women. On the other hand, the English departments in these schools always had more female teachers.

Are men drawn more often to teaching history, civics and economics? Are they more interested in these topics in general? I cannot say. My interest in history has extended into various niche subjects, including the one for which I am somewhat known, the study of "lost synagogues." I have written three books and various articles on the subject, document them in an ongoing blog on Facebook, lead tours, and have been on TV and radio, discussing this historic topic. Yet my Facebook page does not list my name so it is not obvious that a woman is running this page.

Because of this, I have gotten a number of messages and inquiries from people who assumed that a man ran the page, supplied the photographs and text, and ran the tours. I have chuckled at that assumption, but in truth it has irked me a bit. At least a few people have thought that my name, Ellen, was a variation on "Allen" because it is apparently too odd to certain people that a woman is the force behind a lost synagogues research study.

Gender roles can be stifling or liberating, depending upon one's attitudes and orientation and the particular situations we face. I suppose the way I have navigated this throughout my life is to embrace them to a certain extent, and then pursue my interests whether or not they are strictly "female." Though I gently mocked some of the individualistic messages I received as a kid, such as the 1970s *Free To Be...You and Me* songs and TV show, they really did make a strong impression on me. Growing up with models of children and adults making their own choices about activities and clothing, living in diverse New York City, and being exposed to a wide variety of books was exciting to me. I realized that I could like and dislike various things, and even though people could suggest I do certain things based on my gender, in the long run I would have to make choices for myself; it was part of growing up.

Really, beyond a few obvious roles such as child-bearing and bathroom use, I am the kind of person who feels that gender roles are largely artificial constructs. In this day and age, each person travels this road in their own way, with guideposts but also with their own imprint. Some of us feel more comfortable with traditional gender norms, and some of us feel more compelled not to stick to strict scripts. I am not a wildly unusual public figure, nor am I ultra-conformist; I see myself as somewhere in that hard-to-define middle. And happily so.

The Lady in Lime-Green

Rebecca Galin

Mine's no different than the one on *his* head (except for, perhaps, in brightness of color).

What? Have you never seen a woman this Jewish before? I put my kippah on just like everybody else—one hair clip at a time.

I am tired of your stares; I am tired of your rejection.

I say, "Good Shabbos!"
and then "Shabbat Shalom!"
because I grew up Reform
and because I don't want to be Ashkenormative.

But then I say "Good Shabbos" because I want to be seen
as part of the group.

But you do not respond.
I say it a little louder to the next man and he glares back at me
    beneath his black hat.

"I keep a kosher kitchen!"
I want to yell.
"I'm waiting till my wedding night!
I'm carrying this pie in the eruv,
And I'm going to make a minyan!"

I say "Shavua Tov," and the man just scans my body with his
   eyes.
Yes, my skirt is above my knee, but my shoulders are covered and
   so is my collarbone and—
Oh wait! Why do I care about *your* modesty standards?
I am my own person and he's in his 80s and
Am I making him uncomfortable because we're in this elevator
   alone?
And why am I thinking about *his* comfort and F the patriarchy
and feminism! and modesty! and
I'm at the fifth floor.

"You shouldn't wear a kippah"
   he told me, this leader at the kosher food co-op.
"You shouldn't wear a kippah,
   It shouldn't matter if people can tell you're Jewish. That's the
      wrong reason,"
   he said.

"Can't you just cover your head another way? Isn't it supposed to
   be between you and God?"

"Why does it have to be a kippah?"
"You shouldn't wear it to an Orthodox shul,
   not unless you wear it everywhere."

But then why don't *you* just wear a baseball hat? Isn't it supposed
   to be between you and God?

"What about a tallit?" I ask.

"But you're not married and only married people wear them—
see—you don't know enough to be making these choices. It's
not fair to make the other people uncomfortable when you
don't even know."

*It's not fair to make the other people uncomfortable when you don't
even know.*

I do not wear a kippah in my Jswipe photos.
I do say that I want to become a rabbi.
Is that why I have no matches?
There is a shidduch crisis
for halakhic egalitarian Jews too, you know.

I would take out a classified ad if I thought it would help.

Wanted: a nice Jewish boy, a feminist, comfortable being a
rabbi's husband, musical talent a plus.

I'll be the lady in the lime-green kippah
waiting to schmooze with you at kiddush.

Falling in Love with Tefillin

Alona Weimer

one morning, last spring,
I first witnessed an ex-yeshiva boy wrap tefillin

late to our friend's father's yahrtzeit—
egalitarian shacharit on a Tuesday—
he was distracted, fidgeting.

not yet ready to wrap,
I sat back,
watching, listening.
soaking it all in,
I stood witness.

he kept adjusting
the black leather
bound by its obligatory nature.
struggling, stuck,
hardly even praying.
tighten, loosen, tighten again.

perhaps it was then
that I fell in love with tefillin

through appreciation
for my partner's body,
spiritual struggle,

early mornings,
the power of prayer.

thankful for that moment,
for being witness
to manifestations of spiritual struggle.

for through him I am better able
to appreciate the beauty of my own.

Bound

Talia Kaplan

Taamod, Aviva Laya bat Reuven haCohen v'Bracha Shayna
Taking my place at the foot of the mountain,
I enter the covenant
Not yet aware it binds.

Bind them as a sign upon your hand
...a reminder above your eyes
Eyes fixed on masculine lines
from black that binds
How many points for finding a Nice Jewish Boy?
wrapped in tefillin
Me,
wrapped in his arms
My arms,
smooth, unbound.

Taamod
My bat mitzvah tallit with the Jerusalem skyline
Lies in its bag most Saturdays
"Why aren't you wearing your tallit?"
Rabbi's reminder reinvokes the covenant.

Bound by my commitment to Women of the Wall,
to the soon-to-be-women running through synagogue halls,
I wrap myself in the tallit.
But in Krakow and Jerusalem,

I leave my tallit at home.
I wonder if the boys required to wrap tefillin
got the memo about egalitarianism.

In the beginning, Adams before Eves,
Patriarchs precede matriarchs,
Generations of women canonized as "wife."
Is this my lineage?
I'm told Rashi's daughters wrapped tefillin,
but I never see my mother wrap tefillin.
I never see my father wrap tefillin.

My father, who lent me his tefillin
because he's "not religious enough."
"Not religious enough."
A man once questioned my choice to wrap tefillin,
fixated on my flirtation with halakha.
Does the man with tefillin on the city sidewalk—
the man who doesn't look at me—
Ask every man he sees if he observes halakha?
     counts each of the 613 mitzvot?
          davens the full Amidah?

Amidahs A and B
Genesis One and Two
More than one embodiment of the word Jew
And my body should not determine my place.
Who do we allow to take up space
in the history books?

More than one embodiment of the word Jew

And when I say Jew,
I mean the Miriams and the Deborahs,
Rashi's daughters, Puah Rakovsky, Emma Goldman,
Rabbi Regina Jonas, Ruth Bader Ginsburg,
Sheryl Sandberg, Yavilah McCoy, Rabbi Jill Jacobs,
I mean my foremothers
and all those who see them as more than mothers.
I mean *my* mothers:
Bonnie, Sylvia, and Carol. My namesakes, Thelma and Leah.

On January 5, 2017, called to the Torah, I embrace
the name of my foremothers
from my mothers
 bind them as a sign
  codify the covenant

Taamod, Talia Laya bat Bracha Shayna v'Reuven haCohen
Hineini.

I... I'm sorry

Jina Davidovich

A note from Eve to Adam on the occasion of her escape from
   Eden:

Dear Adam,

I've been writing this for hours
Since the moment that God breathed life into me.

After my first bite of knowledge
When my eyes were opened to possibilities
Beyond being ribbed for your pleasure
Beyond the ceilings that the world is bound to set upon the
   dreams
Of the women who will come after me
Beyond the boundaries of this garden
Where Life and Wisdom exist as central forbidden entities
Forcing me to deny my hunger for fruit that will do more
Than nourish these bones, grow these breasts
Make me bleed as I wax and wane
Through a life as nothing more than your helpmate
The receptacle for your biological need to procreate.

I wrote you apology after apology
Crumpling letters whose seeds will likely grow into Trees of
   Doubt
Under whose shadow all young women will blossom

Stretching toward sunlight like a promise
That seems always to elude their thirsty petals.
Some women will spend their lives wondering how it feels to be
warm
Wondering how it feels to do something other than apologize
For the space their bodies occupy
In a world where they have been told that their raised voices
Sound like a betrayal of their femininity
Women, after all, were not meant to speak truth to power
But to listen to men explain the world
Do a twirl in her heels
Mimicking the feeling of her future spinning so fast
That it falls away from the gravitational pull of her dreams
Starts orbiting around a world where she doesn't even have the
time to ask
How it got to be this way.

But not today.
Today is my first day of creation
Today when God asks where I am
You can say that I am free
Seeking out a place where someone will hear
Even when I don't begin with "I'm sorry"
Not sorry for my voice, not sorry for the tree
Not sorry for wanting more.

More than this anatomy
More than birthing children with their father's name
The child of Adam—the First Man—
And Eve: The Great Apologist
Sprouting a human race that will bear my curse

Future women who will feel this same pain
The pangs of childbirth pale in comparison
To the scratches you'd find on the inside of every woman's throat
Generations of apologies that have been clawing their way out
Escaping like smoke from the fire in her belly
Sneaking out past a tongue made submissive and
Landing on frowning lips
When she's asked why she isn't smiling.

Every morning she reads that she was made according to God's
  will
And still she says sorry
סליחה שעשני אישה—sorry that you made me a woman

But today is the first day of my creation story.
And on the first day,
Eve separated the woman from her apologies.
שעשני קדושה—you made me holy
שעשני בכוונה—you made me with intentionality
שעשני בת חורין—you made me free
שעשני רעבה—you made me hungry
שעשני בת שאלה—you made me with the ability to ask
Unapologetically
To want wholeheartedly
To be more than a goddamn metaphor of a woman
Whose greatest legacy is eating from a tree
When you and I both know that my original sin
Was thinking I could use my mouth
To do something other than say *sorry*.

But what did you expect when you named me the mother of all

living things?
Living things need to breathe
To moan
To take pleasure in the rise and fall of our breasts
To feel fireworks explode like orgasms in our minds.
To live under the yoke of apology
Could not be what God intended when
She made this body in Her image.

So I must go.
Leaving a life filled with *I'm sorrys*
Maybe one day they will become stars
In a galaxy
Where each woman is a master over
More than a garden of apologies.

Freely yours,

Eve

Synonyms

Jennifer Brenis

I ran out of ways to say, "being a woman is hard" a long time ago.
I have been the butt of jokes for years,
The punchline in a story about the bra-burning feminist.
And I kicked my feet
And I bit my tongue
And I learned how to say my name without it coming out
   sounding like an apology.

I will never understand why my gender is a controversy
Why my identity is a question
Why the way I was born is unfortunate.
When I was in the fifth grade we took turns leading Hallel for
   the whole elementary school and I never bothered to notice
   that that was the last time anyone ever willingly let me lead
   without making me feel like I was a mistake.

My community preaches acceptance and love and that
women have no place in Simchat Torah.
And there is no greater metaphor for being taught my place in
   the community than me losing the love for what once was my
   favorite holiday.
Because it doesn't seem to matter that I uprooted my life for this
   Torah,
left my family behind for this Torah, but
God forbid I should dance with this Torah.

I don't think we're doing this right
I don't think this is what God wanted from us when they said, "a
    light unto the nations."
God asked us to be good and honest and kind and
follow their laws and change and evolve and
move forward.

Spoken Torah, differentiated as such,
It's in the name,
Only written so we could remember to pull it forward, not
    choose to keep it ever the same.
Speak it
Let it flow like the language we use to express it
Learn it and amend it and let it grow as a vine over the face of
    your life as God wanted us to.

I have been treated the "other" from my conception
And sometimes I feel like my fight is running out of steam and I
    almost want to let it.
And then I hear Simone de Beauvoir in my head
"This is an inauspicious road, for he who takes it—passive, lost,
    ruined, becomes henceforth the creature of another will...
    it is an easy road; on it one avoids the strain involved in
    undertaking an authentic existence."
And I look up new ways to say "hard" and "women" and "being."

Final moments before Yom Kippur

Alona Weimer

it is the final day of the days of awe.
I have been reflecting on the past year's journey,
the ebb and flow of my connection to prayer and peoplehood.

a year ago, a dear friend bought me a siddur.
it was an entrance.

reconnecting to tradition seems radical.
seems gendered.

letting my community teach me seems radical.
seems diminishing of what I already know.

letting love leave seems radical.
letting love stay seems even more so.
how can we navigate loving our womanly selves
while also loving prayer to a gendered god?

how can we incorporate tradition and ritual
while still holding the traditions and rituals
that make us our own?

so many questions for myself this new year.
so many questions for hashem.

about growth,

and all the transgressions I re-committed.

may it be your will.
my will.
that this new year,
I continue to be me—only
braver and better.

Potato Kugel Love

Mirel

I want to lay my whole self
down in the sludge
of my past history.
Scrape and scrabble
in the soil of
my ancestor's best intentions.
To find treasure—
God,
Gold,
or worthless dust,
the bitter agony
of self-deprivation,
ironclad discipline,
and breathtaking withholding.

Worthless dust.
"From dust thou came and to dust thou willst return,"
    but not before you allowed
the forbidden seed to spill,
maybe in the shower when you thought
you were safe from God's eyes.
Or when you were sixteen and you felt you would explode with
    obsessive thoughts.
Maybe you, a young girl, modest and demure in long skirts and
    thick stockings,
let loose and laughed out loud one day because you thought

your gut would burst
with untold pent-up mirth.
And maybe that kind of forbidden laughter became addictive.

Maybe in the great endless suffocating miasma of forbidden
and disallowed,
you kicked your shoes off, unrolled your socks,
and bared your naked, fourteen-year-old feet near the big rock
in the center of Battery Park.
And heart pounding,
Unfamiliar fire throbbing,
dipped your bare immodest toes in the water of a fountain.

Maybe you cried,
sad in the middle of a Shabbat morning,
when, while, drowning in a pool of fragrant
potato kugel love, you felt
a bottomless sorrow well up from inside you.
Hidden from the watchers in your secret psyche, and
untouched by potato kugel joy.
Maybe you self-flagellated and pronounced your soul unsalvage-
    able
because one day you allowed your eyes
to stray at the billboard over Times Square.
You saw two women with large white teeth and bare chests and
    shoulders
gazing into the distance
intent on spilling their cleavage and their secrets to the world.
    Newport! Alive with Pleasure!
Pleasure? What was that?

You hated yourself.
But only because it was so much easier
than to hate the source of your suffering—
The Mysterious

Unbendable
Distant
All Knowing
God.

He who seemed to hold the key to the prison cell of your
  existence.

I want to lay myself down in the mud
of my youthful unveiling and awakening dawn.
Of the delicate unfurling of sexual me.
I want to lay in the mud of my yesterday self and breathe in the
  magic
of the birth of my spirit and the rising of my soul.
It is clean;
It is pure;

It is dirty;
It is sinful;
It is all me,

and will be for good.
And for the rest of my sorry and meager journey
on Earth.

This Eden

Anonymous

blessed am i
entered into the covenant, the coven
of those who came before me
who held and enveloped and allowed us
to go, to roam
to be fruitful, to multiply
to soar on the wings of the Shekhinah
(She who blessed you and me to arrive at this moment)

our first kiss may have been illicit
but the stars seemed to allow it
when you pulled me close
tasted the nervous on my lips
the hesitancy to leap
i haven't stopped falling since

blessed are the stars
peeking between branches
as we fuck in the forest
blessed are your hands
touching me, coaxing me over the precipice
blessed are the golden shadows
illuminating your silhouette
in the afterglow of my touch
under that canopy of trees blanketing our sins

our voices trip on edges
spill down our bodies
syrupy sweet begging to be the same carnal flesh
to be flushed with the blush
of you sinning inside me—
i'd recite shehechiyanu
if i let that wish be our now
if i hold out my hands, allow us to sanctify our sins

Touching Boy

Rivka Cohen

They told me it was against the Torah to touch boys, so I didn't touch boys.

Everyone else touched boys, but **I** didn't touch boys.

"You don't look shomer."

"You don't act shomer."

"You don't dress shomer."

"I wish you weren't shomer," said an anonymous Shabbat-o-gram at an NCSY Shabbaton.

"You're such a tease," said many to my face.

But I liked it. I liked the attention. And anyway, I was better than them—because **I** was following the Torah.

I had many fantasies about what my wedding night would be like. I wasn't thinking about sex, because that was too scary to think about—but I fantasized about my wedding night, when I would finally have my first kiss...

Well, it didn't quite happen like that. It turns out that it's a lot easier to "not touch boys" than it is to not touch "boy." My first boyfriend. A month of summer camp in which we **pretended** we weren't touching as we lay stargazing on the grass or sat talking on a bench. Well, he pretended. I kept scooting over and he kept scooting closer and I kept scooting over and he kept scooting—"Hey, sweetie, I'm falling off the bench." "Oh, sorry."

It took nine weeks. That's over two months since our relationship officially started until I intentionally touched my boyfriend.

I thought that because we were shomer, abiding by the laws of yichud were superfluous.

But as we sat so close I could feel his breath on my skin, I noticed his arm quivering as it stretched behind me on the couch, just barely touching my shoulders.

I let my head drop on his shoulder. He let his arm drop on mine.

I BROKE SHOMER.

I was shomer and I broke it.

I was shomer and I was **broken**.

So I went for it. A voice in my head said, "Don't stop." "You already broke shomer, so why stop?" "You may never do this again, keep going."

We didn't actually go very far. Yet I still had a stomach ache of guilt for three days. And I still had a voice in my head saying, "You're already broken, so why stop there?"

But when I did go further? Pleasure stopped me. Pleasure became associated with guilt. And so I had developed new boundaries for myself, not based on religion or personal conviction or rationality, but based on the guilt of my own pleasure.

On the other hand, I still considered myself shomer negiah. The shame would be too much to bear otherwise. Being shomer negiah defined me. I was still better than everyone else because it still defined me, right? Because I still "guarded my touch."

I still didn't touch boys; I just touched…boy.

Love on the Brain

Talia Lakritz

Sex therapist Ian Kerner writes in *Passionista: The Empowered Woman's Guide to Pleasure* that the brain is humankind's largest, most powerful sex organ. For most of my life, it was the only one I had.

As a lifestyle reporter, I covered sexual health, pleasure, and wellness while actively repressing my own sexuality as an unmarried religious woman.

You can find articles under my name with titles like "5 ways to have the best sex of your life" and "A sex expert reveals 4 products that will help you have better sex." I wrote about intercourse without ever having had it. I wrote about the best lubricants without ever having used them. I wrote about the importance of communication in intimate relationships without ever having been in one.

Luckily, the job of a journalist is not to be the expert. It's knowing what to ask the experts and how to write a compelling story with what they tell you.

I did my research, of course. I gave myself the sex education I never received in my Bais Yaakov high school. I attended sex education expos where the press packets came with condoms. I read books like *Sex That Works* and *Curvy Girl Sex* and interviewed the authors. I attended classes at sex toy shops like Babeland and The Pleasure Chest, and attended a two-week online summit about sexuality and identity called Explore More. I took notes, recorded interviews, collected business cards.

I was, to borrow a term coined by sex educator Reid Mihalko, a "sex geek." I was geeky about sex in the way science fiction fans are geeky about Star Wars—enthralled and obsessed with it, but knowing all the while that it wasn't actually part of my reality.

A recent college graduate in my mid-twenties, I had yet to forge a meaningful romantic connection with anyone. Being shomer negiah wasn't particularly challenging because I felt no pull or desire to break it. Sexual intimacy existed only in theory, reserved for an eventual marriage to a partner I had no concept of.

I harbored crushes. I bought a vibrator. I fantasized about embarking on casual hookups just to see what all the hype was about. But expressing my sexuality in a real way didn't seem possible.

And then I met someone.

He was slender and lean, wearing a turquoise t-shirt and fitted jeans, with wavy golden hair that flopped adorably above his eyebrows. His open, friendly expression was offset by dark brown eyes.

Immediately, I was drawn to him. I felt safe in his gentle yet confident presence, in the unassuming way he carried himself. I just wanted to keep talking to him.

I daydreamed about how lovely it would be to be on the receiving end of his affections, to have that steady, caring attention directed at me.

And then, after weeks of flirting and evenings spent together, it was.

"I've never kissed anyone before, so I might not be very good at it," I told him.

"Really?" he asked in surprise.

"Really," I whispered. "But you're welcome to try."

With no hesitation, he scooted over to my side of the couch, cradled my face with one of his palms, and gently placed his lips on mine.

I remember thinking that this is what skydiving must feel like, when, after meticulous preparations and a steady climb, you finally tip over the edge of the plane and let yourself fall.

His closeness, the explosion of sensation—I didn't realize how sensitive my lips were, how tender another's would feel against them. I closed my eyes.

"Are you okay?" he asked.

"Yes," I said.

"You have to tell me if anything makes you uncomfortable or if you want to stop. Promise?"

"Yes."

His mouth was sweet, smooth and soft like whipped cream contrasted by the coarse brush of his stubble against my cheek. I opened my eyes and saw that his were closed.

He's enjoying this, I thought.

I'm enjoying this, I thought.

Stop thinking, I thought.

And I pressed my lips to his.

What They Don't Tell You About Getting Married at Nineteen

Ayala Tiefenbrunn

"Mazal Tov!"

Mazal Tov, a word that flooded my screens, my voicemail box, the greetings that followed me in every Jewish space I went into. Good Luck.

Good Luck? Are you wishing me good luck? Are you saying that I have good luck?

What does marriage have to do with luck? Didn't Hashem look at me and my husband before I was born and tell us "Listen, you're gonna get married. It's gonna be awesome. Now go be people."

My marriage was written into the backend of the universe long before this ring was on my finger.

I began to resent those "mazal tovs" because that phrase doesn't really seem to mean anything anymore. A beige, vague Jewish platitude that seems inconsistent with the philosophies of divine order.

And listen, I know what you're going to say—"mazal tov" also is a wish of future goodness, but your Yiddish accent, tongue clicking, eyes constantly rolling mazal tovs don't display that. It's more for you own sake than for mine.

"You're Getting Married. Wow."

Like most modern kallahs I went to the pharmacy soon after I got engaged and picked up a pack of pills with instructions that I read online a million times before it was actually sitting before me, and I cried.

This stupid packet of tiny pills, making fun of me. You wanted to finish college. You weren't interested in dating.

Sadly, the perfect man just had to come along at the absolute soonest time. They say the right man is just around the corner, but my right man was practically standing at arrivals in JFK after my return flight from seminary with a giant sign saying "MARRY ME."

No. That's not how it happened. That's crazy. It's a metaphor. I met him less than two months later, but that's not the point, is it?

It was soon. Fast. Not what I expected to happen. But it did. And I was sitting on my childhood bed with a packet of pills that I knew would be in every suitcase I will pack for years. How do you tell your parents, who tried to have children for more time than you have been alive, that you're just gonna hit the pause button for a while?

Tangentially, they were very cool with it, but that doesn't stop them from gasping every time I say I have a good news. Tangentially, I cry every time I see a friend who I haven't seen in a few months and she's sporting a baby bump. Tangentially, I "forget" to take my birth control all the time to make sure that Hashem is OK with our plan.

And it's stupid. Let me tell you how dumb it is, because even if I took every single pill that month at the exact same time, if Hashem wanted me to have a baby I would be pregnant.

And for heaven's sake, there is absolutely no reason for me to be worried about infertility or my biological clock ticking.

I'm fine.

"Are You Going to Finish School?"

My first day of school as a married woman I went to my school's Chabad office to say hello. I was relatively involved the year before and was hoping to continue.

"Oh Ayala! Hi! What are you doing here?" said the advisor.

"It's the first day of school; I just came to say hi and see how your summer was."

"Oh. I just thought because you got married you wouldn't be coming back to school anymore."

I walked out. I was shaking, screaming in my head. I vowed to never go back (and I didn't). I see her around every once in a while and I am filled with rage all over again.

Something about that moment made me start blurting out all the time "I'm not pregnant" or "I'm on birth control" anytime anyone even slightly suggested the idea of me having children. Children would mean I was giving up. As much as I find joy in cooking and cleaning, I am not a housewife. I did not apply, get accepted, and attend one of the premier design schools in the country just to drop out. I realized in that moment that as a Jewish woman, my choice to get married at nineteen would always overshadow my hundreds of other choices. I could never be serious enough, goal oriented enough, creative enough to be taken seriously by other Jewish women because I got married so young. I had to let everyone know that I "had my priorities straight" by taking birth control.

"But You're A Baby!"

Every once in a while we have Shabbat guests who spend their entire time in our home laughing at us because of our age. They look at our clean home, beautiful Shabbat table and delicious food, and they're freaked out. How could a couple that got married so young be so put together? Let's just say we have a blacklist.

Most women in my circles are not married at 22, not pregnant at 22.

Many of my friends are older than me. I'm currently living a life that was "meant" for someone older than me. And it doesn't help when people are judgmental as opposed to helpful.

I get that age is just a number. Trust me.

But I wish that other people did too.

"You're So Frum!"

Heterosexual, monogamous sex is the holiest thing a person could do.

With their spouse.

To have a baby.

But every month that goes by I'm at the mikveh and I know in about 30 days I'll be back here. Naked, cold, and just wanting to not come back for a while.

And it won't feel like I'm baring anything or shedding a layer of tumah because if niddah is marking the potential life that didn't come to fruition, does knowing you're not ovulating make this entire process meaningless?

But no life has passed. Just 28 little pills.

Growing Pains

Anonymous

We were married for a month before we successfully had penetrative sex. Not for a lack of trying on our part, but because each attempt ended with me in tears, unable to understand why my body wasn't working the way my kallah teacher had said it would.

That first time, I lay there as my husband managed to achieve full penetration—finally—and tried desperately to hold in the tears of pain. Every few moments, my new husband looked at me and said, "I'm going to stop. It's hurting you." And each time I replied, "Don't. I'm fine. Please."

I wasn't fine at all, and the tears swimming in my eyes were all the proof he needed. He stopped.

I bled immediately afterwards, and I kept bleeding. After three weeks, I finally mustered up the courage to go to my gynecologist. She attributed the bleeding to my new birth control and the painful sex as "growing pains." I tried to explain that my vagina seemed to shut down whenever we tried to have penetrative sex, and that I suspected it was more than "growing pains" but she, a frum woman herself, knew better and sent me on my way with a prescription that read: "Buy a water-based lubricant."

And so we tried again. We had used lube the many times we tried, but maybe what my body needed was specifically "water-based." I held on to that hope as I checked out at Duane Reade, bottle of KY Jelly in hand. I texted my husband and told him we had to try it out tonight. The doctor said it would work, that this was what my body needed to work. It had to work.

It didn't work. I sighed as I said to my husband, "Maybe I'm just nervous. Let's try again tomorrow." But the same thing happened the following night. By the third night, I was sobbing into my pillowcase, shaking with anger and sadness at my pathetic, broken body. I emailed my gynecologist and told her that the lube wasn't working. She wrote back an hour later: "Try more lube!"

I made an appointment to see her the following week. Each night we continued to try, sometimes with success, but always with a pain that felt like my body was being torn apart.

And in a way, it was.

My kallah teacher, my friends, and the frum community that I trusted had led me to believe that my body would know "just what to do" when the time came. I was promised that by "waiting until marriage," I'd ensure that our sex life was far more meaningful and sacred than for those who had premarital sex. I was promised that any first-time pain would quickly vanish in the face of heightened joy and ecstasy with my new husband.

The reality of the situation, though, was much different than what I had been led to expect. I was a failure. Every single tear, every ounce of frustration, every whispered apology to my extraordinarily kind and patient husband was a manifestation of the ongoing damage to my spirit. My body failed me. It failed us. With each attempt, I began to believe that I was less of a woman, and certainly less of a wife than I wanted to be.

My return visit to the doctor yielded new information: "Your vagina is atrophied. Basically, it's shriveled up like a raisin. We don't usually see that in women until they hit menopause but it's such an easy fix... I'll give you an estrogen gel that'll clear it right up."

A weight was lifted off my shoulders—finally, an answer! And a cure. I dutifully picked up the yellow and pink boxed medication which cheerfully spoke of all the ways that menopause wouldn't change my life. I inserted the medication night after night, carefully following their instructions to avoid any sexual contact while using the gel.

One week later, at my follow up appointment, my gynecologist told me that my vagina was stubborn and that I'd need another week's worth of medicine. "Feel free to start trying again at the end of this round! If you're feeling better, you don't even need to come back. Oh, and if this doesn't work, maybe you should consider going on Xanax or something to help you chill out."

I was giddy with anticipation. Each night after I inserted the medicine, I counted down the days until we could resume trying. The last night of the medication, I cheerfully told my husband that the following day was the first day of the rest of our lives. He laughed, happy to see me optimistic.

The following night we tried again. I waited expectantly for my newly cured vagina to give way and let my husband enter me in the way he should have been able to on our wedding night. "It feels like there's a wall," he said, using a description we'd both grown familiar with. It didn't hurt quite as much, but penetration was near impossible. A few more half-hearted attempts and we gave up. I didn't even cry. I was so deflated that I just crawled into bed and fell asleep.

My Orthodox friends never spoke about their sex lives, and I wasn't comfortable asking their advice. But I am blessed with good friends who are not Orthodox, and when they asked how our sex life was six months after our wedding, I shrugged and said we didn't really have one. I told them I was still having "first-time" pains, and it made it hard to have sex. I told them I figured it'd take a little while but eventually it would get better.

Shortly afterwards, they staged an intervention. "We know you don't talk about this where you're from, but this isn't normal. Go to a new doctor. Find out what's wrong, because something *is* wrong."

I found a new gynecologist. At our first appointment, I sat in the chair and cried: "My last doctor told me that my vagina was atrophied but she gave me meds and they fixed the atrophy but my body still doesn't work and it hurts so much and I hate myself and my body and I think I should just tell my husband to divorce me because he's never gonna be able to have a regular life with me. Please can you tell me what's wrong with me?"

She sat with me and talked me through a battery of exams, both internal and external. She told me that I had vaginismus and vulvodynia, and prescribed a topical painkiller and referred me to a pelvic floor physical therapist.

Armed with a diagnosis, I logged onto my computer and began the first of many Google searches. I learned that vaginismus made the muscles of my vagina contract involuntarily, making prolonged penetration impossible. I learned that vulvodynia was chronic pain around the vulva with no identifiable cause but which lasts for longer than three months. I learned that many thousands of women are misdiagnosed each year, while many more are told that there's nothing wrong with them.

I learned that these diagnoses are most common in two groups: Indian women and evangelical Christian women. The medical literature is sparse, but what does exist suggests that these diagnoses are more common in populations where sex is treated as something negative and shameful.

Though my teachers would disagree (they *did* say that sex within marriage was beautiful and husbands were required to sexually satisfy their wives), I spent the first two-and-a-half decades of my life being told that sex—that any touch between the sexes—was bad and shameful. It's hard to flip a switch on that mentality just because I had a ring on my finger.

I started seeing a pelvic floor physical therapist shortly after that appointment, and began seeing a licensed sex therapist. I knew that the physical problems were largely a manifestation of emotional and mental blockages related to sexuality, and I wanted to address the issues head on.

I loved my physical therapist and our weekly sessions, despite the fact that they caused me tremendous discomfort. Each week, my physical therapist stuck her fingers inside my vagina, pressing down on my muscles to decrease the tightness and teach my body to be comfortable with foreign objects inside me. I had to use a series of dilators, each bigger than the next, to continue this exposure therapy at home. None of this was covered by my insurance, which considers vaginismus and vulvodynia unnecessary problems to treat.

With my sex therapist, I began to uncover the emotional and mental entanglements that made sex impossible for me. In sessions alone and in sessions with my husband, we explored the meaning of shomer negiah in my life, the dictate to "wait until marriage," the shame I associated with sex, and what it might mean to live a life different than the way I grew up.

Slowly, I began to heal.

Four years later, I'm proud to say that my husband and I have the sex life we were promised in our kallah and chatan classes. My teachers were wrong about many things, but they were definitely right about one thing: sex does mean so much more when you have to wait—and work—for it.

One Day, This Scar Will Be Beautiful

Hannah Dreyfus

Sometimes, I stand in front of the mirror and trace the red horizontal scar directly above my pubic bone. Scars, like memories, fade with time. I will wait patiently. My scar is still tender and pink. The memories still ache.

Several months after the birth of my son, I went to an OB/GYN who specializes in VBAC deliveries—a vaginal birth after cesarean. I did not go because I wanted to have another baby anytime soon. I went because I needed someone in a white coat to tell me that what I had gone through was not my fault. I wanted someone to tell me that maybe, someday, I could have the birth I had spent months envisioning, ticking off the details in the purple boxes of my birth plan.

Ina May Gaskin, considered by many the "mother" of modern midwifery and credited with launching the modern home-birthing movement, made me a tall promise she couldn't keep. I, like many other expectant moms, spent afternoons leafing through her *Guide to Childbirth*, a natural childbirth manifesto. Ina May told me to leave my inhibitions and fears about childbirth at the door. She told me to rebrand contractions—they would be "rushes"—and the pain would be lost in the anticipation, the euphoria of the moment. Ina May told me that sex and childbirth were really only a hairsbreadth apart—an orgasmic birth, if I did it all right, was possible.

I wanted to do it right. Childbirth, I thought, was a chance to conquer my body. The insecurities that plagued me—stretch marks and achy knees and swollen legs—would fall away in sweeping rush after sweeping rush. I would emerge, victorious.

And then there would be the moment of meeting my baby. I would hold his warm body against my chest while the chord still throbbed, attaching me forever to that first, breathing moment.

Instead, I remember numbness. I remember hearing my baby's heart rate start to drop on the monitor, a solemn procession of beats that slowed and dipped, then rose only to slow again.

I remember signing the consent form with a shaking hand, as my husband put on scrubs. I didn't recognize the signature on those papers—it was not a discernible name, just a scribble. Mine would be the fifth c-section of the day, the nurse anesthetist told me.

When they hoisted me onto the operating table, they asked me to help shift my weight. My legs felt like coal. I willed myself to move my body, but could not. My limbs, hours before writhing in pain as I fought through hours of labor, felt heavy and futile. My thoughts, too, fell limp.

Under the white lights of the operating table, I listened to the nurses discuss their most recent vacation to the Caribbean. "Wish I was back there on the beach," said one face, leaning over me. "Beats being back here in this awful heat."

I felt close to God in that moment. Closer to God, I dare say, than in the many months that followed, when exhaustion, loneliness, and a constant, imperious anxiety demanded all of my energies. On the operating table, under white lights that scorched my tired gaze, I recited an age-old Psalm written by King David, the passionate poet and fallen hero. "Though I walk through the valley of the shadow of death, I fear no evil, for you are with me."

* * *

I did not die. Death, really, had never been a thought. I got out of bed the evening of my surgery, determined to walk. With hospital gown gaping at the back, I shuffled my way down the hallway of the labor and delivery ward, past the healthy baby nursery, with its cheerful nurses and neatly bundled babies, to the neonatal intensive care unit where my son was placed.

With my long, unkempt hair swept up in a hasty ponytail, I lowered my frame into a rocking chair and placed my son's tiny warm hand on my chest. Breastfeeding had always been my plan, but my body was too swollen, his mouth too small. Still bloated from the water they had pumped into my veins through an IV during the nine hours of labor that preceded my surgery, I felt oversized, as if looking at myself through a funhouse mirror.

The nurse tried to coax him onto my breast. "If you hold him like this, and just push his head like this." He whimpered. I handed him back to the nurse. "I'll come back and try again next feed," I said, voice hoarse. Hoisting myself out of the rocking chair, I hobbled back to my hospital room, waving goodbye to my small son through the NICU's swinging glass door.

The rest of my three-day hospital stay remains a blur, with painful, vivid moments coming back into focus. There was the mother with whom I shared my hospital room, who told the nurse she "didn't want to nurse" after her rosy baby latched on without a hitch. There was the first moment my husband and I were alone together since the birth—in a hospital room, with bizarrely colorful artwork on the walls, we sobbed over the grape juice boxes that came with our Kosher meal. It was a Friday night, the Sabbath night, and in the solitude of the hospital room we recited the ritual blessings, choking up in silence from the shock of it all. Side by side we fell asleep—my husband cramped awkwardly on a couch beside my electric bed, where I lay, blinking into the darkness—bandaged, immobile, collapsed into a tower of pillows.

There was the nurse who took the IV out of my wrist, though protocol demanded it be left in place throughout my stay. "You don't need this anymore," she said, removing the tape and the needle from my hand. Surveying the bruise near my vein, I thanked her.

There was the doctor, who came in and told me it had all gone "as well as we could have hoped."

There was the social worker who came in to evaluate me for postpartum depression.

"Have you been crying a lot?"

"Yes."

"Do you feel constantly overwhelmed?"

"Yes."

"Well, try and rest up during the remainder of your stay and if you feel these symptoms getting worse, consult your doctor, OK sweetie?"

And there was the pumping. The every two hours, on-both-sides-for-20-minutes pumping sessions, which I did dutifully after coming back from my NICU visits. This was the only way my milk would come in, the lactation consultant told me, wagging her finger. In the meantime, a bottle would have to do.

I fell asleep hunched over the pump, the brusque whirring and sucking noises continuing undeterred. The bottles, pressed against my breasts so hard that the shields left a circular indentation, remained empty. The few drops of liquid I was able to retrieve were placed in a syringe and chaperoned over to my son in the NICU. It was the first time I bartered for liquid gold.

* * *

This week, 11 months to the day since I left the hospital, I brought my breast pump home from work. I carried it with me on the subway in a bulging red backpack, hoping a stranger would ask. One full year of breastfeeding, against tough odds— my son's initial failure to latch, my breasts' less-than-ideal architecture, a bad bout of mastitis three months in, an oversupply that didn't allow me to sleep through the night, and, of course, the immense logistical challenges that accompany any full-time working mom's decision to breastfeed.

I deserved a party, maybe, or a certificate. I imagined the elaborate celebrations that might sufficiently recognize a year of lonely visits to that cold back office, three times a day hooking myself up to that whirring machine, now a curmudgeonly old friend.

But somehow, there was no time for celebrations as I rushed into the evening activities that had hardened into routine. Bath time, playtime, bedtime, clean-up, lunch prep, bedtime. Rinse, repeat.

With my son's first birthday rapidly approaching, I sat down at my computer to write. What, I asked myself, did I have to add to the milieu of mommy commentary that came before me? I had devoured stories of other moms processing dramatic, unpredicted and often traumatic births. I had burrowed deep into Google's hallowed corridors with inquiries about milk supply, postpartum anxiety and clogged ducts. I had scrolled through Instagram photos of moms celebrating their postpartum stretch marks and wobbly midriffs. That would be me, one day, I told myself. I would love this body. The uneven pink line over my pubic bone would become a battle scar.

In the dark and uncertain months that followed my birth, I

longed for an elegant resolution. A moment when I vanquished the feelings of insufficiency that mocked me from the shadows. A moment when the vivid fears of something, everything going wrong—fears that pressed up against me in a crowded subway car during my morning commute—would smile, apologize, and melt away.

I longed to feel triumphant, vindicated. The way Ina May told me I would feel, when I conquered my fears and surrendered to my carnal instincts. Then, only then, I would open, I would rush, I would flow.

That moment never came. When I trace my scar, I still feel pain. I still feel robbed of the moment I so badly wanted—the privilege of being fully present to greet my son when he entered the world. I still cry when I think of the numbness that was mine instead. When I remember the sleepless nights, trying to coax my wailing son onto the breast I pleadingly offered him, I still bury my head in my hands. The frustration, the despair I felt towards a body that seemed to have failed me—these memories remain, subdued but not forgotten.

One year later, I have learned that it is okay to mourn this loss. I have learned that while others do not always have the right things to say, sometimes empathy matters more. I have learned that owning up to the loss of anything—a dream, a hope, a vision of how things ought to have been—takes time, but is a necessary part of healing. I have learned that grieving for the experience you lost is independent from appreciating the healthy child you have.

I have learned to fight the voices that deride and ridicule my imperfect body, for the weight that might never come off, and the problematic breasts, and the pelvis that started it all.

In that way, I remain a student of Ina May, steadfast in my

belief that this body has the power to overcome.

Scars, I have realized, are not meant to disappear.

Immersion

Anonymous

I stared at myself in the full-length mirror, naked. I didn't feel pretty exactly. But I felt honest—stripped of my makeup, the suit jacket I'd worn to work that day, a purple paisley dress, my best Monday try at confident posture. I searched the slope of my back for separations, the corners of my eyes for rogue mascara. I scrutinized every inch of skin, blotchy and red from the hot shower. I'd never really looked at myself before. I grinned as if at a stranger.

How did I get here?

It had to be a rhetorical question, because nobody knew I was here. I didn't tell my boyfriend. I knew he wouldn't understand—why I needed this, how some ancient bath ritual could make me feel clean. He was religious too, but didn't grow up that way. *The Magic Touch* never sat on his bookshelf next to *The Berenstain Bears* and *Harry Potter*. Gila Manolson never stood on his shoulder, clucking, exasperated.

"So, you want to bring God into the bedroom?" he asked once. "That's why you haven't slept with anyone? That's why we're waiting?"

"Yep. Pretty much."

He let out a slow, tired whistle.

Turned his lips up in the echo of a smile for my benefit.

I couldn't tell my friends where I was either. My virginity was an assumption I didn't protest. So was my sex positivity. I went to the *Vagina Monologues* every year. I swapped Notorious RBG memes. I cheered on my friends' Tinder misadventures. They thought I was too progressive to carry around all that shame, the guilt of offering up my recycled body to a mythic future husband, the fear of divine disappointment.

But I also volunteered at shul. I blasted Shwekey with non-ironic abandon. I patiently endured 40-Year-Old Virgin jokes through my college years. They thought I was too Orthodox to be there, peeling off clothes in a nondescript building ritually preparing myself for an ordinary Monday, not my wedding day.

Too feminist for a purity complex, too frum for sex. It was the perfect dual image to avoid questions—or new labels, like the one I'd assigned myself: hypocrite.

A knock.

I walked to the edge of the pool, the edge of a precipice. I wasn't sure I wanted what could happen later: the vulnerability, the loss, the finality of it. I wasn't sure I didn't.

"It's time. I can make this holy," repeated in my head like a prayer. "I can make this holy, holy, holy..."

I dunked, humming the niggun of my father's rebbe. My eyes burned. I wasn't sure if I was crying.

Tahor, tahor, tahor.

Pure.

I breathed. It felt like the first time.

Private Places

Sarah J. Ricklan

These are private places. But the evening is dark, so my husband walks with me. I walk alone in this town during the day, but it's so dark in the evening. I don't like walking alone in the dark. Last time I did this, it was daytime. Last time I did this, it was a thousand miles away. We walk together to the house. I see the sign. Large enough to read, small enough to be discreet. You wouldn't know unless you knew. My husband checks that I'm all right.

"I'll text you when I'm finished."

"I'll meet you back here." I watch him dash around the corner, because this is a woman's space.

I ring the bell. A woman's voice answers, and I tell her I have an appointment. She sounds flustered. She opens the gate. "I just have someone finishing up. Would you mind...?" She looks around, asking me wordlessly if I would wait out here. I won't, not in the dark, not in the cold. And my hair is wet. She realizes this, and invites me into the antechamber. "You can sit here, and I'll tell the woman finishing up that you're here." This attendant knows these are private places. She doesn't want us to see each other. She wants to preserve the anonymity.

She goes into the other room, maneuvering her pregnant belly through the doorway. But the room is not soundproof, so I hear the conversation. "I don't want to rush you; take your time. There is someone waiting outside, so just let me know when you are ready to leave." I think I recognize the voice that responds. It's a small town.

A few moments later, the woman emerges, wearing a scarf around her wet hair. I didn't know she covered it. I was right about her identity. She chats to me for a moment, tells me she tried to make the bathroom tidy. The attendant seems surprised that the woman did not want the anonymity. Did I?

I go into the preparation room. The attendant asks me what I normally do, and what I would like her to do. I have no normal; it's only my second time. I tell her this. So we decide together that she will check my back for stray hairs. I go in and shower, making sure to breathe, remembering the last time I did this, last month, a few days before my wedding. I was with my mother. She's back home, thousands of miles from here, and as I comb through my hair one more time, I miss her.

I expected nothing of that first time, when I went with my mom. If anything, I expected to feel resentful about being shackled—shackling myself—into an ancient menstrual taboo. I felt that resentment, that sharp, debilitating sting that comes with realizing what womanhood in my world seemed to mean, when I stood in the bathroom and performed my first hefsek tahara, an internal check to make sure I had stopped bleeding. These are private moments where only rabbis' words intrude and instruct me to wrap a piece of cloth around my index finger, squat, and check myself. Only rabbis' *words* make me wear white underwear for the next seven days, and do some more internal checks. Only rabbis' words can make me *clean*. But they're just words, right? No *one* transgresses my private places. I could stop listening, couldn't I? I have shackled myself.

But I did not feel that resentment when I immersed in the mikveh for the first time. I choose not to describe what I actually felt, but it was something powerful, positive, that I never thought I'd feel. But these are private places, private feelings.

These private feelings made me excited, in some sense, for this second journey into the water, this second visit. I wanted the chance to thank my God. I wanted to pray about my life and my marriage naked and wet. So I leave the preparation room, and the attendant checks my back. She holds up a towel as I enter the water. A curious practice, I think. Small modesty in full nudity. I sink myself into the water and breathe again.

Ready.

Dunk.

When I emerge, I say the blessing.

"Amen." I am reminded that I am not alone.

I breathe.

Ready.

Dunk.

When I emerge this time, I take a vulnerable moment to think, to pray. I have not yet memorized the prayer I want to say, so I blabber to my God. My words surprised me. Praying naked with the sounds of water lapping against the walls feels rare, as if I must lap up every moment, make every word count. It is my one chance to pray in a ritual space that is not shul. I feel simultaneously free to speak and aware that I will not have this moment for another month. I'd better make it count.

And then I remember that I am not alone.

It's hard to pray on one's own with someone else behind you.

So I finish, breathe, close my eyes. Ready, I suppose. When I emerge finally, I take one last short moment, and then climb the stairs. My towel is waiting.

In the preparation room, I text my husband. *Ready.* And I walk back outside, my wet hair cold in the dark night, and take my husband's hand.

Glossary

Amidah—One of the main and central parts of daily prayer, said at every prayer service

Ashkenormative—Denoting a world view that promotes Eastern European Jewish (Ashkenazi) customs and traditions as the normal or preferred form of Judaism

Bat mitzvah—Jewish coming of age ceremony for girls, celebrated at age 12 or 13

Chabad—An Orthodox Jewish Hasidic movement, known for its outreach activities, with hubs on college campuses and throughout the world

Chatan—Groom

Chazal—An acronym for "Chakhameinu Zikhronam Livrakha," meaning "Our Sages, may their memories be blessed," referring to the Jewish sages of the Oral Law

Erev—Evening, or, when used in the context of Shabbat or a holiday, the day before Shabbat or the holiday starts

Eruv—A boundary that symbolically extends the private domain of Jewish households into public areas, which allows observant Jews to carry items in public on Shabbat

Frum, frumkeit—Religiously observant, religious observance

Halakha, halakhic—Jewish law, pertaining to Jewish law

Hallel—A set of prayers comprised of Psalms 113-118, recited on Jewish holidays and the first day of each month

Hashem—God

Hefsek tahara—A ritual internal check that a woman performs at the end of her menstrual period to confirm that she has stopped bleeding

Hineini—"Here I am;" this is the response Abraham gave when

God called on him to sacrifice his son Isaac; other Biblical figures also use this response when God addresses them

Kallah—Bride

Kallah teacher—A person, usually a woman, who teaches a bride about the Jewish laws concerning sex, menstruation, and ritual purity

Kiddush—A blessing over wine to sanctify Shabbat; also refers to a communal gathering over food immediately following Shabbat morning services

Kippah—Skullcap or yarmulka

Mikveh—A bath used for ritual immersion in Judaism to achieve ritual purity; observant Jewish women typically immerse before marriage and after each menstrual cycle

Minyan—A quorum of ten Jewish men or ten Jewish adults (depending on the sect of Judaism) required for traditional Jewish communal prayer

Mishkan—Tabernacle; a portable spiritual sanctuary for God

Moshe—Moses

Niddah—Menstruation; "in niddah" is also used to describe the state of being ritually impure during the menstrual period

Niggun—A wordless melody

Rashi—Acronym for "Rabbi Shlomo Yitzchaki," one of the most influential Jewish commentators on the Bible and Talmud who lived in the 11th to 12th centuries

Rebbe—Rabbi; pronunciation often associated with Hasidic sects

Shacharit—The morning prayers

Shavua tov—A greeting that means "have a good week," offered after Shabbat ends

Shekhina—The feminine divine presence of God

Shehechiyanu—"Who has given us life;" a blessing recited on special occasions and for new experiences

Shidduch, shidduch dating—A match for marriage; a dating system in which single Jews are introduced to one another through matchmakers, for the purpose of marriage

Shomer negiah—Observance of the prohibition against touching a member of the opposite sex (other than a spouse)

Shul—Synagogue

Siddur—Prayer book

Simchat Torah—Jewish holiday celebrating completing the yearly reading of the Torah; the holiday is celebrated in part by dancing with the Torah, and everyone who is eligible to recite the Torah blessings in the synagogue is called up to do so

Taamod—Feminine conjugation of "stand up;" used when calling up a woman to read from the Torah

Tahor—Ritually pure; status of purity obtained by immersing in a mikveh

Tallit—A fringed shawl worn during morning prayers

Tefillin—Phylacteries; a pair of black boxes containing Hebrew parchment scrolls with black leather straps attached; one box is placed on the head and the other is wrapped around the arm

Tumah—Ritual impurity; often associated with menstruation, which renders a woman ritually impure until she immerses in a mikveh

Tzniut, tzanua—Modesty, modest; often refers to clothing and behavior

Yahrtzeit—The anniversary of someone's death

Yarmulka—Skullcap or kippah

Yichud—A Jewish law prohibiting the seclusion of an unmarried man and woman together, to prevent them from being tempted to have sex

Zera l'vatala—The "wasting" of sperm typically associated with male masturbation

Acknowledgements

We would like to thank the countless people who enabled this book to come into being, from the very inception of the project through its publication. First and foremost, we would like to share our deep gratitude to the authors of this book, the brave and beautiful women who opened up their hearts and shone light on their most private experiences. You are the lifeblood of this project, and needless to say, without you, this book would not have been possible.

We would also like to thank the many people who were instrumental in supporting *Monologues from the Makom* when it was just a small event in someone's living room. Thank you to Eve Ensler, playwright of *The Vagina Monologues*, for inspiring this project and helping us realize the power of personal narrative as a form of activism to transform culture. Thank you to the trailblazing Jewish feminists who came before us, who led the way in creating a community where this project is possible. Thank you to the amazing women who hosted, performed at, and attended those first events, and thank you to everyone who has since shown such enthusiasm for the project. You showed us and told us that this forum was important, that *Monologues from the Makom* was something our community needed and wanted. It is because of your positivity, love, and energy that this project ever got off the ground.

Thank you to the people who made this book a reality. To Amalya Sherman, thank you for your bold and stunning cover art. To Rabbanit Dasi Fruchter, we thank you for your moving words of framing and introduction. Thank you Dr. Joy Ladin, Rabbanit Leah Sarna, Chaim Trachtman, MD, and Professor

Lisa Fishbain-Joffe for acting as early readers of the book and for your kind words of encouragement. Thank you to Larry Yudelson for your guidance and publishing prowess.

We want to offer our deepest gratitude to our families. Thank you to our parents who have always supported us, helping us become the women we are today—to Roberta Weinstein-Cohen and Mark Cohen, Marjorie and Jordan Hirsch, Deborah Mehl and David Ricklan, Paula and Leibel Rozner, and the Weitzmans and the Zimilovers—we thank you for your love and support. Thank you to our partners and spouses—Eliezer Lawrence, Elliot Salinger, and Ilan Weitzman—for sharing and supporting our visions for a more just world. And to Rebecca's son, Nadav Weitzman, who came into this world during the creation of this project, we thank you for inspiring us to foster a better world for future generations of feminist girls and boys.

Finally, we would like to thank God, in all of the complexity of our varying relationships, for granting us life, passion, and power. We offer this book as an act of prayer for a world of justice and love.

About the Editors

Rivka Cohen is the Director of Partnerships at Lissan, a non-profit promoting linguistic justice for Arab women in East Jerusalem. She previously served as the Program Manager at JOFA, the Jewish Orthodox Feminist Alliance. Rivka has spoken about her travels and experiences at Jewish conferences and retreats, in sessions entitled, "A Jewess in Morocco" and "Unlearning Sex Negativity." Rivka is passionate about interfaith relations, Jewish community building, and feminism.

Naima Hirsch is a writer, educator, and life-long student. She has studied Torah and Talmud at Nishmat and Drisha, and Creative Writing at Hunter College. Her work has been published in Alma, Hevria, and Germ Magazine. As she begins studying for rabbinic ordination at Yeshivat Maharat, she hopes to continue shaping the discussion around sexuality within the Orthodox community.

Sara Rozner Lawrence is a Clinical Psychology doctoral student at Fairleigh Dickinson University and a long-time sex education enthusiast. She currently serves as the moderator of the Joy of Text, a monthly podcast about Judaism and sexuality. Sara's undergraduate research on Orthodox women's comfort levels with sexuality was presented at the annual meeting of the Society for Behavioral Medicine in 2017, and she remains passionate about furthering research about sexuality and sexual stigma in the Orthodox community.

Sarah J. Ricklan is a medical student at NYU Grossman School of Medicine. Her academic interests and research involve the evolution of human childbirth, maternal health, and healthcare access. She was drawn to *Monologues from the Makom* because she is interested in investigating how women's health and Orthodox Judaism inform and complicate each other.

Rebecca Zimilover works in community engagement and fundraising at one of the largest local philanthropies in the world. She holds a Master of Social Work from Columbia University and a Master's in Jewish Studies from the Jewish Theological Seminary. Rebecca's interest in this project originated in the systemic lack of openness to femininity, feminism, and sex education in her Modern Orthodox yeshiva background. The lessons of *Monologues* have taken on even greater importance in her newest role: Mom. She lives in Riverdale, New York with her husband, son, and their pup, Sabra.

Also available from Ben Yehuda Press

Life on the Fringes:
A feminist journey toward
traditional rabbinic ordination
by Haviva Ner-David

"With no holds barred, Ner-David touches on all the
issues of the day: women and Jewish study and ritual,
Jewish attitudes towards hetero- and homosexuality, and
the tensions between generations. Many of the scenes in
this book will not soon be forgotten."
— Samuel Heilman, author of *The People of the Book*

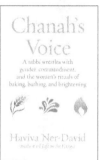

Chanah's Voice:
A rabbi wrestles with gender, commandment,
and the women's mitzvot of
baking, bathing and brightening
by Haviva Ner-David

"I have always admired Haviva. I loved her first book, yet
Chanah's Voice is more remarkable. It is not only a unique
contribution to the literature of feminism and Orthodoxy
but also a significant work that better fits the categories of
the theology and social anthropology than autobiography."
—Blu Greenberg, author, *On Women and Judaism: A View from
Tradition*

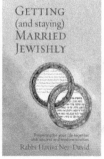

Getting (and Staying) Married Jewishly:
Preparing for your life together
with ancient and modern wisdom
by Haviva Ner-David

"Haviva's special guide for engaged couples helped us both
order and frame some of the hardest conversations we've
yet to have, while the activities/exercises often allowed us
to surprise each other. Having this book to help us prepare
for our wedding and marriage was truly a blessing."
—Viki Bedo

CPSIA information can be obtained
at www.ICGtesting.com
Printed in the USA
BVHW070617050920
588144BV00001B/11

9 781934 730041